Denise Del Cruz
4022 City N. Paulina
Chicago Il. 60613
935-4362

Sex Objects in the Sky

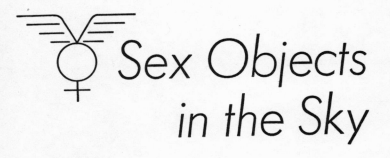

Sex Objects in the Sky

A Personal Account of the Stewardess Rebellion

BY PAULA KANE
WITH CHRISTOPHER CHANDLER

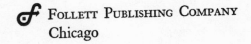

FOLLETT PUBLISHING COMPANY
Chicago

Library of Congress Catalog Card Number: 74–80327

ISBN: 0–695–80485–5

First Printing

TO JAN WINN AND DENISE DeCLUE

Contents

Thanks to Jan Taylor, Donald Dunn, Neil McBride and the many members of Stewardesses for Women's Rights for making this book possible.

Young and pretty, the slaves of the harem are always the same in the sultan's embrace.

Simone de Beauvoir
The Second Sex

Sex Objects in the Sky

The Flying Dream Machine

WHAT is that pretty young stewardess thinking as she walks gracefully down the aisle to get you your third drink?

Is she anxious, as much of the airlines' advertising says, to "Make You Feel Good All Over," to be asked "Almost Anything"?

Or is she perhaps musing about last night's orgy, as films such as *The Swinging Stewardess* and *Come Fly With Me* would suggest?

If she is a stewardess who has been flying for some time, the chances are very good that she is only hoping that someone won't make a pass at her or get drunk and make a scene.

The airlines have used stewardesses to create a flying dream machine, so that male customers can indulge their sexual fantasies instead of feeling afraid or insecure while in the air. But stewardesses, the objects of these fantasies, can only live in this never-never land for so long. Then they become disillusioned, angry, rebellious. And once they begin to live in the real world, life on the airlines suddenly seems bizarre.

Judy Caroll is a stewardess for TWA. Last June on a flight from New York to Chicago, a distinguished looking gray-haired, black-suited passenger asked her to please reach up and get his coat from the overhead rack. As she did, she felt a pinch on the behind. Later in the flight another passenger, seated near the distinguished looking gentleman, asked her if she would get his hat from the overhead rack. She reached up and the same elderly gentleman slipped his hand up her skirt.

To his surprise the "sweet young thing" turned on him, fixed him with a stoney glare and declared loudly, "Sir! Do you have your hand up my dress?" There was a stunned silence, as every passenger strained to see what was happening. The silence was broken by the voice of his wife declaring, "Harry, I told you to keep your hands off the girls!" as she hit him with her knitting needles.

This is one example of what seems to be the eternal American love triangle: scolding wife, fantasizing husband, delightful young sex object. It's also an example of a new attitude of defiance and self-respect on the part of the object of fantasy.

What is it like to be that flying sex object? The carefree envy of women, the sexual fantasy for men? I was a stewardess for American Airlines for five years, and now, nearly a year after I quit, I am just beginning to understand what happened to me during those years.

I can see now that the airlines have carefully constructed the airborne fantasy world. Advertisements always picture the submissive geisha girl service on board. Stewardess colleges teach us how to think of ourselves as models or cocktail waitresses, totally self-absorbed in our makeup, our way of walking, our hairstyle. We are judged and evaluated on the job on the basis of our dress, our smiles, and letters from satisfied customers.

The image of the stewardess has taken its place right next to the Playboy Bunny in our national psyche. Different airlines have created different scripts for their women, from the blond bombshells of Pacific Southwest to the girls-next-door of United. But we all share the basics. We are supposed to be the fresh, wholesome girls who love men, the quiet concubines of the pilots, and the submissive partners to male sexual fantasies.

I recently met a former Playboy Bunny who recalled that in the midst of her more ardent amorous exploits she always had in the back of her mind that this was nothing compared with what the stewardesses were up to.

I remember sitting on my jump seat on a plane, facing the passengers and leaning into the aisle to see a whole row of men staring at my legs. Or escaping into the galley, the one place on the plane which is your own turf, where you don't have to be on stage as a performer, and the men coming up, leaning casually against the door, trying to pick me up. "Nice day," they would say, "Where are you going tonight?" or "You girls sure work, don't you?"

Then there was the casual patting of my behind as I walked down the aisle, the assumption in a hotel elevator that because I had a uniform on, I was somehow public property, to be joked with, sidled up to. The expectation was that I would have to be nice, because the fellow passenger in the elevator was a customer or a potential customer.

One of the worst experiences that I had in this regard involved a public relations man for my own company. It was on one of those junkets that the airlines regularly throw for press people. They were supposed to be promoting travel to Mexico, but it was really just a drunken airplane joyride. After about ten free drinks this one PR executive began intimidating all of the eight stewardesses on board, ordering them around in a snotty, uppity way. I was busy taking another passenger's order when he came up to me, grabbed me by the front of my hair, and pulled me toward him. "Pretty face," he said sexily, as if this was supposed to flatter me, or turn me on. It didn't. I was disgusted, perspiring, and boiling over. But I said nothing. I just held my breath and stared at him till my eyes filled up with tears of rage. Finally he cast me aside.

By the end of the flight this obnoxious clod had purposefully hit two stewardesses with his garment bag, shoved one roughly aside, hit another under the eye with his small carry-on, and threatened to have another fired because of her bad attitude.

Our brave flight service director talked with him afterwards and came back to inform us that we didn't have to worry about anything. He was not going to report us. Everyone of the stewardesses wrote a report about him, but we were ignored.

Aside from the occasional extreme cases like this one, there were many instances of drunk and rowdy passengers, and regularly on commuter flights there would be at least one passenger who would get absolutely irate and throw some kind of temper tantrum. I think that this probably happens because we stewardesses fail to live up to their expectations. We just don't fulfill the myth.

Yet the stewardess fantasy has become embedded in the national psyche. Men dream of escaping their families for a few days of romantic freedom to another city, perhaps picking up a stewardess on the way. I even know two married, seemingly well adjusted men who get physically aroused at the thought of flying. And I've heard men brag of achieving what they consider the ultimate "score," the fulfillment of the prurient dream: they claim they made love to a stewardess in the plane lavatory. I'm sure they were only dreaming.

Almost lost in all the sexual innuendo of the Madison Avenue imagery is the primary reason why stewardesses are on board a plane, which is to enforce safety regulations and supervise the immediate evacuation of the plane in the event of a crash. And in crash after crash, the efficiency and courage of the stewardesses have meant the difference between passengers' lives and deaths.

Forty passengers and three crew members were killed in the December 8, 1972, crash of a United Airlines jet at Chicago's Midway Airport. But fifteen passengers survived, many of them because of the heroic efforts of the two stewardesses, Kathleen S. Duret and D. Jeanne Griffin.

The plane crashed into a block of houses one and a half miles southeast of the runway while attempting an instrument landing in scattered fog. Almost the entire front end of the plane was demolished on impact. The two stewardesses, who had been seated in jump seats at the back of the plane, rushed to open an emergency exit, but were driven back by raging flames. They worked their way along the right side of the burning cabin, clearing away the debris of galley equipment blocking the aisle. Then, one by one, they assisted nine surviving passengers to the exit and out of the plane, pausing each time to take gasps of fresh air before returning to the dark, burning, smoke-filled cabin. Six passengers found their own way out through breaks in the plane's fuselage.

The National Transportation Safety Board found in its investigation of the accident that most of the passengers in the cabin section died after impact as a result of inhaling carbon monoxide and other poisonous fumes from the fire. Those nine passengers lived because of the experience, the expertise, and the courage of Ms. Griffin, a stewardess for ten years prior to the accident, and Ms. Duret, a stewardess for seven years.

Yet their actions earned just one sentence in the sixty-one-page NTSB report: "Nine passengers who exited through the rear service door were assisted by the two flight attendants; these attendants were the last to leave the aircraft."

Their exceptional bravery in carrying out their legal

role on the plane, as stated in Federal Aviation Regulation 121.391, "to provide the most effective egress of passengers in the event of an emergency evacuation," earned them no citations or awards from the airline.

Stewardesses who please customers, who receive complimentary letters, and provide exceptional "service," receive awards of merit from the airline. But apparently not stewardesses who save human lives.

You have entered the weird, upside down, Alice-in-Wonderland world of the airlines. Presumably the companies are very concerned about safety, since the public's concern for safety on planes has been a major problem in attracting more customers. Yet in several areas the airlines display an incredible disregard for elemental safety. Hazardous materials are illegally shipped in cargo bins below the passengers' seats. Cabins are constructed with materials that in accidents emit a deadly, cyanide-filled smoke.

The stewardesses, in charge of safety in the cabin, are dolled up in miniskirts and coonskin caps, "hot pants," and other bizarre costumes. They are seated in unsafe jump seats, in unsafe corners of the plane, are always called "girls," and are treated like children by the company. And when they "grow up," they are encouraged to leave, even forced out after flying a few years, because they are no longer considered girlish enough.

The tightly written script they are ordered to act out in the air, including the constant smiles, the constant engaging of each customer's eyes, the constant subser-

vience, makes it difficult and sometimes impossible for
them to enforce even rudimentary discipline during the
flight.

The sexual stewardess fantasy has a direct effect on the
safety of flying. It also takes its toll on the psyches of the
women who play the role. Stewardesses tend to have serious identity problems as a result of being treated like
pieces of fluffy assembly line equipment by the airlines.
We tend to move in regular stages from romantic idealism
to disillusionment to frustration and anger and self-doubt.

Until recently that was the end of the line. The disillusioned, angry stewardess would quit. The companies,
fully realizing the syndrome, arranged for average tenure
to be from eighteen months to two years. They had what
Kelly Rueck, head of the largest stewardess union, calls
the corporate policy of "use them 'till their smiles wear
out, then get rid of them and get a new bunch."

But in the past few years stewardesses have finally
started to fight back. They have won a series of rulings by
the Equal Employment Opportunity Commission that
have stopped the airlines from forcing women to retire
from flying at an early age and from banning married
flight attendants.

Since these rulings were issued average tenure has
grown from two years to more than four years, and is
increasing every year. Stewardesses on some airlines have
gained the right to maternity leaves and full career pen-
sion benefits, and there is a movement afoot to make
stewardesses federally licensed, like other members of the
flight crew.

Male stewards were employed on every airline as a result of another EEOC ruling, and several female pilots were hired during 1973. The legal groundwork has been laid for sweeping changes in sexual roles on airplanes.

But the airlines haven't given up. Since the first anti-discrimination actions were filed in the mid-60's, the airlines have produced their most sex-oriented advertising, have for the first time dolled up their stewardesses in couture costumes, and have introduced novelties such as the in-flight "air strip" fashion show. They seem prepared to retrench and fight a last-ditch battle to hold on to their stewardesses as flying geisha girls.

It's shaping up as a giant battle of the sexes in the skies. Arrayed against the airlines are groups such as the fledgling Stewardesses for Women's Rights, a new, nationwide organization dedicated to improving stewardesses' working conditions and status; and Mary Poppins, an ad hoc organization of older, more experienced stewardesses. Joining in the struggle are the labor unions, sleeping giants that have only started to wake up to the issues of professionalism and dignity.

They are lined up against the formidable powers of the major airlines—powers of public relations and image making and political clout. They are opposing the imagery of the stereotyped sexual roles, an effort that is seriously threatening to the self-image of a lot of people. Even a respected reporter like Harry Reasoner seems to feel threatened. I remember him saying on his regular TV broadcast that he was opposed to union efforts to guarantee full career benefits for stewardesses. He said he preferred "young and attractive" women on his flights. "The surly union women," he suggested, should be replaced by "soft and fluffy ones."

But change is inevitable. There are forces at work that cannot be stopped by PR gimmickry or male fantasy. The "soft and fluffy" young stewardesses joining the airlines these days don't put up with the same kind of abuse that we did five years ago. The male stewards, now making up as much as 20 percent of the enrollment at flight attendant schools, put up with even less. These young people are determined to make a dignified, professional career out of flying, and the older stewardesses, with experience and seniority, have decided not to be forced out by the airlines' end runs around age discrimination laws.

The airlines are fighting a losing battle, because of anti-discrimination laws that are now firmly established, and because sexual roles are undergoing a general metamorphosis in our culture. The whole imagery of the virile pilot and his submissive, geisha girl stewardesses is already a relic of the past.

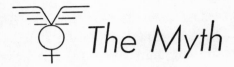 The Myth

STEWARDESSES are supposed to lead the most glamorous of lives. They date movie stars and baseball players. They hang out at the Playboy mansions in Chicago and Los Angeles. They attend bizarre, ultrahip sex parties. If you can believe the television special based on the book, *Coffee, Tea, or Me?* they sometimes even have a husband in every port.

The whole profession revolves around the glamor myth: it is why some women join the airlines; it is how the stewardess is perceived by passengers; and it is often how stewardesses perceive themselves.

Like most myths, it contains some elements of truth. A few stewardesses get into the Vegas scene or the baseball scene or the Playboy scene. Some feel a kind of personal breakthrough from their Victorian past, and briefly enter a new, seemingly free world of choice and sexual experimentation.

But for the most part the myth comes down to impersonal associations with the famous and the influential, usually by way of providing an attractive, nonsexual escort service.

One stewardess for American Airlines is often escorted by Cary Grant, appearing at restaurants and nightclubs, keeping him company, and being provided with her separate bedroom every night.

A friend of TWA stewardess Jan Taylor was entertained by the Prince of Saudi Arabia during a layover in London, and actually was introduced to the king. Jan recalls wondering at the time why nothing like that ever happened to her.

Nothing quite so glamorous ever happened to me either, but there certainly were times when we all felt we were leading the most exciting and free and interesting lives in the world. For me it was a two-month period during my first year, when I was flying a regular trip to Mexico City, staying at the best hotel there, and being wined and dined by Mexican men who thought stewardesses came from another world.

For most stewardesses the glamor wears off fast. For a few, probably those who tend to be the most attractive and the most adventuresome and who receive the most rewards from their role, the myth lives on.

Sally Morgan is one of the very few stewardesses who has come close to actually living up to the image of the glamorous, carefree "stew" who flits around the world being wined and dined and loved by exciting men. She has dated baseball players and movie stars and entertainers in Las Vegas. She is exceptionally good looking, with rusty red hair, and she flies for TWA. In 1973 she was selected as "Miss Chicago Interline," the beauty queen of the airline club, and was rewarded with numerous free passes for two. Her life seems to run at a frantic pace.

"I have been skiing in Switzerland, I've gone shopping in Hong Kong, and have ridden around on the back of a motorbike in Acapulco," she says with pride.

"My roommates and I met Jerry Lewis on a flight, and he invited us to Boston where he was having a performance. So we went, and he ended up giving us his suite. He treated us like three daughters.

"We were sitting in the front row for his show wearing pant suits, so the next day he sent us shopping to get dresses. He treated us like precious little angels. It was fun."

She describes how she got into Las Vegas late one night and took a cab to a casino where Glenn Campbell was playing—how she got in free and was invited backstage between performances.

And how Chuck Berry has shown her his collection of polaroid pictures of stewardesses—some 100 candid shots including his prizes, a stewardess bending over in the galley and another sitting on the captain's lap.

Recently she had a blind date with a movie star, arranged by a producer who was dating her friend, Anna. She said she was hoping it would be Paul Newman, but it turned out to be the man who plays a doctor on a television series. They all ended up at Jack Webb's house in L.A. for a party.

Her friend Anna Truit also flies for TWA. She is

blond, very pretty, and self-confident. She has dated base-ball players and movie producers and entertainers, and introduced several of her friends into the Playboy, Las Vegas, and Hollywood scenes. She and her friend Patty were both pictured in a *Newsweek* magazine article about Hugh Hefner, but she considers Hefner's Playboy man-sion a pretty dull place.

"Every Sunday when Hefner's in town he puts on an afternoon brunch and a movie, by invitation only. It's mostly girls—we can invite other girls, but not guys. Most of the people are very plastic, wearing the latest mod fashions and anxious to be more 'in' than anyone else. But the food is excellent, and the mansion is a sight to behold.

"At about five minutes to seven Hefner comes into the room and that is the signal that the movie is about to begin. He sits down in a large, two-person center chair with a girl—last time it was some blond girl—and the butlers serve popcorn and cakes all through the movie.

"One night we sat up with Hef and Barbie until about 3 A.M. playing 'Sorry.' Hefner wanted to stay up and play 'Clue,' but we all left. He was really upset because people wanted to leave. He's used to people staying around for his amusement."

Both Sally and Anna are leading somewhat quieter lives now. But shortly before I interviewed them they had both become involved in an unusual game with a man they met on a flight to Los Angeles.

He was a very large, flamboyant man, about 40, weighing some 300 pounds, with longish hair and bushy side-burns. He wore platform shoes, a huge bow tie, and glasses with wide gold frames engraved with his initials. A gold Aries medallion dangled from his neck.

He struck up a conversation with the four stewardesses on the flight by showing them pictures in a gift catalog and asking them if they would like the gifts. Finally he invited all four out to dinner.

At supper he gave them each a cocktail ring, and proposed that they play an elaborate game. He would take each of them out and shower them with gifts. The only rules would be that the stewardess could stop the game anytime she wanted to, and that the four women were not allowed to talk to each other about him.

The four, including Sally and Anna, agreed to play the game.

Sally said he took her shopping twice. He bought her a ruby ring and expensive clothes.

"I quit the game when he wanted to move into my apartment a few days a month," she said. "He said he would buy all the furniture for my new apartment if he could spend a couple of nights a month there.

"I told him, 'Here's where I stop.'"

Sally had mixed feelings about the whole episode. She said he was a "strange man who got off on showering gifts."

"He's a very warm, genuine person, but he's lonely. I think he is very much in need of love.

"The last couple of days he's been with Anna," she

said. She seemed a little anxious. I think she was feeling competitive, wondering if Anna was getting more presents.

I talked with Anna a few days later, and she confirmed that Sally was the only one to have dropped out of the game.

"I really liked him as a person," she said. "Physically he doesn't turn me on, and if he ever persisted, and it was bed or bust, I would have to decline."

Anna said he bought her two pants outfits, her stereo set, a pair of shoes, and a purse.

He is seeing one of the group who lives in L.A. these days, she said, and she and Lisa, another Chicago-based game-player, joked the other day about getting off the plane in Los Angeles the next time and seeing the fourth contestant drive up in a Rolls Royce.

She related the joke to the gift buyer, and he too found it amusing, she said.

I found conversations with these women difficult because they seemed to be living so comfortably in a world where people casually exploit each other. I didn't feel like I could criticize their behaviour without shaking their self-confidence. They were so caught up in living the stewardess myth and being exploited as sex objects that they didn't see the classic "sex for money" exchange that was the basis for the game.

Both Sally and Anna seem to have a strong ambivalence about their own lives. Most of the stories they tell sound as if they happened to someone else. After reeling off a whole series of sketchily described adventures with this movie star and that baseball player, Sally unexpectedly said:

"These were all little girl antics. I'm tired of the whirlwind." She said she would never go to another city for a date or a party again.

Anna had similar feelings.

"The first couple of years were wild and freaky," she said. "Then it just becomes another job."

Jan Taylor has an interesting perspective on the workings of the myth. Three years ago Anna brought her along for a wild evening in Las Vegas, complete with front row seats for Buddy Greco and Sammy Davis, Jr., coffee afterwards with Buddy and Sammy, and then the midnight show at Caesar's Palace, and an after-show party in another celebrity's room where everyone smoked marijuana.

Those were the days when Jan was just breaking out of her Victorian past. That summer she was smoking grass, meeting celebrities, and dating a member of the Christy Minstrels.

She also got into the Rush Street scene in Chicago, working part-time as a cocktail waitress at a dating bar called Shenanigans.

"Working at the bar was a natural extension of the stewardess role, which is probably why almost all the barmaids I knew then were stewardesses," she said. "Like on the plane, we were in a position to initiate conversations and respond or not to advances as we wished.

"The difference was that men in the bar tended to be younger and therefore more appealing, and we had far more time for conversation than on a plane.

"In a bar," she continued, "the customers seemed to consider us more in the public domain than passengers do a stewardess, perhaps because there wasn't such a mythic aura about barmaids. But the owners of the bar were far more protective and respectful of us than the airlines. If a man hassled a barmaid he was out on his ear, but if he hassled a stewardess the airlines apologized to him and disciplined her.

"At the time I was really into the game and knew all the tricks.

"I used to wear hot pants—a snazzy little blue knit outfit, with support hose that really made my legs look sexy," she recalled. "I used to be an absolute knockout, with my long hair and long legs. It was a new kind of freedom for me. I could walk up to someone and start talking. I was able to make the advances. It was a natural extension of being a stewardess."

Jan now sees that stage in her life as her means of breaking out of the Puritan ethic of her background, as a stage in developing her own identity, but it certainly wasn't enough.

"It was not a viable alternative to the Puritan ethic," she says. "It was just as devastating, just as exploitive as the old way of being a submissive wife and mother."

It was a way of life that could be described as living in the "Playboy" world, she feels. Hugh Hefner's "Playboy philosophy," espoused in his magazine in a lengthy series, called for a complete freedom from our restrictive, Victorian past. It was typical of the whole advertising and movie heroine myth that has developed over the past twenty years.

But the myth only substituted for Victorian prudishness and subjugation a kind of impersonal body worship of women—women who were unblemished, girlish, passive, obedient picture postcards, women who were the playthings of the elegant rich and powerful and creative. Airline stewardesses were selected and trained to play that role.

Stewardesses like Sally and Anna are among the small group of women who have come the closest to actually living out the myth. But you can't live the myth forever. Both are now struggling to get their lives into perspective. Sally said recently that she has been living at such a hectic pace that she almost didn't know who she was anymore.

Anna felt that there was a period of her life when she was completely out of touch with her own feelings. She was devoid of emotion. To a certain extent we all lose our identity as we try to play out the stewardess role. Many of us are no doubt attracted to the job in the first place because we have questions about our identity, and, at least for a time, we can play the role of stewardess to the hilt. It all seems like a game, a charade, a costumed ball.

But somewhere along the way we come to realize the basic emptiness of the role. I think the realization is hardest to deal with for those who become involved in the kind of casual promiscuity that seems to be called for by the script.

Many of us come from small-town, conservative, and even puritanical backgrounds. This is particularly true for American Airlines, with their "all American girls," and United, with their "girl next door" image. We are raised as the opposite of the myth of the cosmopolitan, sexually-free women that is a portion of the mythology, and we never succeed in playing that part of the role. We remain puritanical, often even virginal, for years of flying. Several of my close friends in Chicago would never go out with a man again if he made any kind of advances on the first several dates. We were looking for friendship above all else, and some of us were playing the old game of trying to trap a wealthy man into marriage.

You make several choices along the way as you start to play out the role of stewardess. You can move into the airline community invariably located by the airport, immediately lowering your expectations, and living in the super-small-town atmosphere of an industry settlement. Or you can venture into the big city to live. If you do, you will almost invariably end up for a time in the dating bar scene—every big city has one.

In Chicago it's on east Division Street, with Butch McGuire's and Mother's heading the prestige list. These are the places where the "regulars," the men's men, wear their women on their arm like an expensive accessory, where the men don't seem to like women's company very much, except as a means of proving their masculinity.

Some stewardesses get trapped in that scene for a long time. One night a close friend of mine, Kathy Hartman, came over to socialize at my apartment after a flight. She was a striking woman, always dressed in the hippest fashions. After we had been talking for some time she suddenly broke down and started crying, cupping her face into her hands and gasping for breath.

"What's wrong with people?" she said. She was becoming more lonely and unhappy every day. Men never called her back. She could never maintain a relationship with a man beyond the first night.

"I read all the articles in *Cosmo*. I buy only the finest of clothes to accent my best features. I spend a fortune on make-up. I can cook a gourmet meal but almost never get the chance to show what a whiz I am in the kitchen.

"When I meet a man I usually end up going home with him, and I guess that part of the reason is that I'm afraid he won't call me back if I don't.

"So we usually end up going to his place and we usually end up in bed. Not that I really want to so much as it is that they want me to.

"I do everything I can. I even fake orgasms."

I didn't really register the significance at the time of what was happening to my friend. There she was, tall, thin, fashionably dressed, a true picture postcard of a beautiful young American stewardess.

Soon afterwards she began dating a man who lived in another city, and they became very close, although he planned to never marry. The last time I talked with her she was living in terror of his finding out about her past. It may have been her way of feeling guilty for transgressions against her puritanical upbringing.

I have several stewardess friends who have reacted to

the depersonalized sex-object role in various ways: one who set out to trap and marry a successful businessman, and succeeded within a year and another who reacted against the sexual suggestiveness of her role by refusing to see any man who might make a pass at her. The second woman ended up forming her closest ties with an alcoholic whom she sometimes had to support because he couldn't keep a job, but who never threatened her sexually.

But Kathy is the worst victim of the mythology. She tried to do everything that was asked of her, to be the perfect sex object, and came closest to succeeding. She had lost almost every last vestige of her own identity. She said that flying was the only job for her—she could never imagine doing anything else.

Thousands of women are stewardesses, and among those thousands there are no doubt many who have a reasonable outside life and have established an identity that has almost nothing to do with their job. There may even be a few who are more successful at living out the sexual aspects of the mythology, who could even be clinically defined as nymphomaniacs. But in five years of flying I have never met one, nor even heard of one.

No, stewardesses just try to hold on to their identity while pretending to play a ridiculous role. And the archetypical stewardess is not found in pornographic movies or girlish adventure stories. Kathy is the ultimate stewardess.

Stewardess College

LIKE so many other small town girls, I thought while I was growing up in Brockton, Massachusetts, that it would be the most wonderful of lives to be an airline stewardess. I applied with two airlines when I reached twenty, but I was not one of the chosen few.

I became a nurse and moved to Boston to work at the Joslin Diabetic Clinic. I roomed with several other nurses and was leading what seemed to be an extraordinarily ordinary life. One Sunday I noticed an ad in the paper with an exotic looking stewardess standing by her baggage, about to take off for unknown lands. I decided to give it one more try, so I cut out the application blank and sent it in.

A few weeks later I had my interview at Boston's Logan Airport. This time I was determined to excel. I wore a red, white, and blue outfit—the colors of American Airlines. During my interview I was as enthusiastic and charming and graceful as I could manage.

My interviewer was an ultraprofessional-looking woman who engaged me in light conversation, measured my hips, and finally handed me a sheaf of papers to sign. The papers said I agreed to work any hours, be stationed in any city, if my application was favorably received, and to quit at age thirty-two.

I was so anxious to get the job that I lurked in the hallway after the interview so that I could ask the next girl interviewed if she had signed anything. She said she hadn't, and I was elated. I had been selected.

I wouldn't have been so excited if I had known the basis on which the airlines select their stewardesses. The standard criteria are looks and character. They are looking for fair young women who will be anxious to please. But it's even worse than that. One flight service supervisor for Eastern Airlines was quoted recently as saying, "We're very interested in a girl's leisure time activities. If she lists reading and knitting as her favorite occupations, she's obviously not the kind we need."

A United executive said, "We need more Indians than chiefs. It'd be hard to keep a lot of high-powered career girls in line. We need the ones who are going to drop out and do something else after a few years. It's only natural."

So I was selected because I didn't read or knit much, and looked like the type who would drop out to get married in a few years? I don't think the recruiters are really all that precise. They seem to look for reasonable looks and something that some of them call the "giving personality."

But the airlines make it sound as if you were selected because of an innate superiority to other, lesser mortals. At our first day of classes in Flight Training School in Fort Worth, Texas, we were told how proud American Airlines was of us, how fortunate we had been to be selected, how we were one in a hundred, all-American girls.

I don't know exactly what I expected in flight training school, but it certainly was not what I got. We supposedly needed to be trained in airplane safety, emergency evacuations, the serving of meals, and other ways to make the passengers comfortable. But the school was more like a crash course for the Miss America pageant. We were forced into a total, narcissistic self-absorption. Girdles, fingernail polish, false eyelashes, ratted hair, makeup, how to walk and sit down and climb stairs— these were our obsessions for the next six weeks.

The airlines have apparently modeled their stewardess schools after the Army's basic training. Many of the same group psychology techniques are used: our hair was cut, our clothes changed, our makeup changed, our walk changed. We came to look like entirely different people.

The setting was in keeping with the image of glamor. The school is a beautiful complex of low, modern buildings set back from the road like a luxury hotel. There are acres of grass and trees, tennis courts, and a swimming pool. The postcards describe it as a "combination health spa and country club." You can't see anything from the estate except the almost deserted, old Fort Worth airport.

The routine of classes was to become excruciatingly

boring for most of us students. About 20 percent of the time was devoted to safety, and 80 percent to grooming, etiquette, and how to serve various meals, including elaborate, first class, multi-course dinners.

The first week we got an idea of what was expected of us. The teachers would go around the class and check our fingernails. If we had the smallest chip in our polish we had to redo our nails. I'm surprised I still have any nails left after the amount of polish remover I poured over them during those six weeks.

Our skirts could not be more than three inches above the knee, and our hair had to be clean and puffy, ratted and teased to give that round "set" look.

The second Monday was the most traumatic day for many of the women in my class. The grooming instructor inspected us, one by one, and told the beauticians what to do with our hair. We had no say in the matter. Our hair was simply cut the way she decided it would look best. At the time the airline favored a short-haired look, and several of the women who had hair down their backs cried that night because their hair had been chopped off. I remember seeing one woman lying across her bed sobbing, her remaining hair frosted and ratted.

When a woman was thrown out of the school it was done suddenly and without explanation. She would be called out of class and no one would ever see her again, so we were never sure what she had done to be eliminated. This caused us all to be anxious to obey all the rules.

We always felt as if someone was watching us. There was speculation that the rooms were bugged, and rumors went around that some of the women were spies to make sure that we really had the right attitude. We were afraid of everything and became anxious to conform and to please.

It was pretty hard to stay awake in classes but we didn't dare fall asleep. Every instructor wore her immaculate uniform and was perfectly groomed. They were all bubbly and enthusiastic. They would often start classes with a funny story about some experience they had as a stewardess. One related how an obstinate passenger had refused to place his attaché case under his seat. She leaned over him, she said, and told him, "There are just two places you can stick that case. One is under that seat."

The class really enjoyed that story. I used the line myself once when I was flying. I said it very politely, of course.

We all pretty much fell into the school's routine after a time. Classes from 9 A.M. to 5 P.M. with a break for lunch. Dinner became the social event of the day, something to be looked forward to as a break in the monotony. The food was excellent, but of course we had to worry about our weight. I am five foot five and my weight limit was 120, which became a continuous struggle when eating was the main pleasure of the day. There were scales all around to remind us of the consequences of overeating.

We learned to master the lip brush, the choice and application of various cosmetic bases, the use of blush highlighting, mascara, eyeliner, and false eyelashes. We learned how to sit down in a chair gracefully by feeling the base of the chair with our heels and easing down, body erect. We learned how to climb stairs, never looking down, bending only at the knee, sliding the ball of our foot gracefully onto each step.

In the evenings there wasn't much to do. We had little money, were a long way from downtown Fort Worth or Dallas, and there was a strict 11 P.M. curfew. We spent most of our evenings practicing our walk, doing our fingernails, exercising in the exercise room, experimenting with makeup, and washing and curling our hair.

There is an awful lot of work involved in always being immaculately clothed and groomed. It requires an almost total concentration on how you look down to the smallest detail of figure, grooming, and dress. It requires hours each day to approximate the image of the clean, healthy, neat, naturally beautiful all-American girl.

It was not an atmosphere that encouraged you to make good friends. But we did try to help each other out. There was one woman in our room who just couldn't seem to get herself organized, so we all pitched in before roomcheck in the mornings to help straighten her things out. Several mornings we just barely made it before inspection, chucking all her things in her closet.

Another woman drank every night, and we'd make sure she was awake in the morning. We'd shake her and get her moving and feed her coffee.

Nobody dared ask where she got her liquor because we didn't want to know. We thought we'd be guilty as accomplices if we knew. Nobody wanted to make waves. Nobody wanted to stick out of the crowd.

Somehow a group of us did meet some students in Dallas, and toward the end of the six weeks we rented a car for the night and went to a party.

On the way back we got lost. Curfew was 1 A.M. Sunday, and we left in plenty of time, driving toward the three towers that we used as a landmark for the school. Somehow we ended up in the middle of three radio towers in the desert.

We knocked on the door of a house near the towers, and a man let us in to use the phone. We called the school and the supervisor on duty said we would have to be there by 1 A.M. or the metal gates would be locked. It was ten minutes to one, and we were all really frightened. The man was very understanding, and he actually got into his own car and led us back to the expressway. Once we got on the expressway he peeled off and we sped by, our frantic driver flooring the gas pedal until we were careening along at ninety miles an hour. There were seven of us crowded into the car. I lay down on the floor of the back seat, figuring that was the safest place to be if we cracked up, and I began to wonder if flight training school could be worth this kind of panic.

We made it back to school just before curfew.

The preparations for graduation began weeks in advance. We were to receive our "wings," a small set of silver wings similar to those awarded pilots after completion of flight training. But the ceremonies reflected the childish atmosphere especially created for us.

Each class elected a "Junior Birdman," who was like a class president. We elected the perfect incarnation of the stewardess image. She was beautiful, blond, adorable, and gung ho. She was always smiling, always happy. We all voted for her, and mumbled among ourselves, "She deserves to be Junior Birdman."

The school took its Junior Birdman very seriously, though.

Her name was added to the bronze plaque on the wall next to the grooming department. The plaque included the names of all the Junior Birdmen that had been elected since the beginning of the school.

We also had to make up songs for our graduation ceremonies. One of our songs was to the melody of "Impossible Dream" from *Man of LaMancha*. The words described the proud stewardesses that served the public on the line. We practiced our songs every night for a week before graduation.

When the day finally came we all wore our uniforms for the first time. The ceremony was held in the front entranceway, with each of us filing by, like in a college graduation ceremony, to have our wings pinned on our chests. Then there was a speech by a visiting executive of the company, and we sang our class songs. We lined up on the huge stairway for our class picture. It was finally over.

I vowed to myself that day that I would always be a law-abiding citizen, because I knew what being in jail felt like. It was not that we had to work hard, or suffer terrible deprivations. It was the fact that we were treated like small children, that we were judged on a whole range of standards that meant nothing to us, that we were being molded into automatons.

I went to flight training school in the spring of 1968, and there have been some changes since then. Some of the airlines, notably United, have changed their training programs, dropping the graduation songs and the curfew.

Most of the other airlines have also dropped their curfews and, with men now attending the schools, are in the process of being forced to modify some of the other, more childish aspects of training. But the script remains essentially the same.

You would think that the airlines would show a little more concern for safety. But the training schools still spend a little over a week of training on safety, and still find plenty of time for modeling and grooming. For instance United Airlines, which has one of the better reputations for safety training, now has the same single week to train flight attendants on nine different aircraft which it had ten years ago when the airline only had two aircraft.

Even a cursory look at the accident reports prepared by the National Transportation Safety Board shows the crucial importance of how stewardesses react in a crash situation. How can the airlines not care?

Similarly, every stewardess can expect to be confronted by medical emergencies, and yet the medical training in flight schools today is minimal, usually two or three hours of first aid, focused on air sickness and other minor ailments.

But the airlines still cling to the childish script. One night recently a class at the flight attendant school of one of the major airlines was practicing its songs for graduation ceremonies when a young stewardess struck up a traditional ditty called "Lap Time," sung to the tune of "Swanee." Most of the class joined in singing:

> Lap time, how I love you, how I love you,
> My dear old lap time.
> I'd give the world to be
> Up in the cockpit
> Sitting on the captain's knee.
> Coffee, cigarettes, and good intentions,
> Don't you believe it.
> The passengers will see me no more
> When I go through that cockpit door.

This is only one of several odes to pilots that we sang when I was in school. But now there are male stewards going through the training program, and they find it difficult to share the same fantasies.

There were ten men in this particular class, and one of them stormed out of the room in the middle of "Lap Time." That night he wrote an angry letter to the school administrator, arguing that the singing of silly songs was demeaning to the profession. The next day he was told he was being dismissed from the school. He did not have the proper attitude.

The Honeymoon

IF a stewardess tells you about one of her exciting escapades, chances are that it happened during her first year of flying. This is the honeymoon, the brief romance that many of us have with flying. There are difficult times, but everything is still new and exciting, and we become enamoured with the glamor of our own lives.

There is the excitement of learning about the special world of stewardesses. There are the "stew zoos," or apartment complexes near the airport that cater especially to flight attendants and their admirers. There are the "stew bums," men who are always extremely polite and gentlemanly with stewardesses, seemingly wanting to do nothing more than accompany us and help us in any way they can.

On our first day in Chicago we ended up in a "stew zoo" near the airport, and were rescued by a "stew bum," who brought us to a much more interesting community on Chicago's lakefront and showed us the apartments available there. This particular stew bum apparently was also a real estate salesman.

We began to learn some of the folklore of flying, and to hear rumors through the airline industry grapevine. It was said that companies selected stewardesses by putting a Hula-Hoop over their heads. If the Hoop stopped at her breasts, she was hired to be one of the busty girls at Pacific Southwest Airlines. If it stopped at her hips she went to TWA, and if it fell all the way to the ground she was an American Airlines stewardess.

We learned that customers to and from New York were by far the most difficult to deal with, the most demanding, and the most drunken. We would hear stories about movie stars on planes who dated stewardesses, or who were accidentally doused with drinks by a nervous flight attendant.

Each month we bid for the flights we would most like, all the way up to 150 possibilities. We had the least seniority, so we were the least likely to win our bids. The trips we usually ended up with were the least desirable—short hops from one small midwestern city to another. But bidding was fun, a way of gambling with fate, and each month we had another chance to win the good life.

This was the time when Jan Taylor went to her one and only wild party in Las Vegas, and started dating a singer with the Christy Minstrels; and when Sally and a girl friend met two New York Yankees at the Apartment Lounge in Kansas City, and on the spur of the moment joined them on their last road trip.

But even in the first few months of excitement there

are difficult times. Three of the twenty-four stewardesses who came to Chicago from our class dropped out during the first three weeks. Four more quit during the first few months, often because they found it unbearably lonely in a strange city, with roommates who were usually out, and sometimes because they could not bear the way they were treated by the passengers or by the company.

One day during my first week of flying we were returning to Chicago from Syracuse with a full load of people, and we were rushed to get everything cleared away before landing. I was almost running down the aisle, dumping the trays into the galley when somehow I got my finger jammed between the two sliding doors of the buffet.

I called to my fellow stewardess, "Hey, I've got my finger stuck." But she just ignored me and kept shoving trays at me. "Please, help me get my finger out of here," I begged.

"Just keep emptying those trays," she said frantically, shoving another load at me. I was kneeling on the floor of the buffet, trying with my free hand to empty and stack the trays, and she kept running in and dumping more trays over me—just throwing them in my general direction.

Somehow I got my hand free before we landed, no thanks to my frenzied friend, but I looked disgusting— absolutely disgusting. My hand was throbbing and swelling up. Egg crumblings were dripping from my face and down my uniform. My nylons were torn and my knees were bruised and black from the dirt on the galley floor. My white shoes were filthy, and I was sopping wet with spilled coffee and perspiration.

So this is what flying was really like! I hid out in the lavatory, trying to clean myself up a little. I couldn't possibly go out to say goodbye to the passengers as they got off. I wouldn't have said goodbye to myself at that point. An agent came on board and knocked on the door and said I would have to get off the plane because passengers were boarding for the next flight. The plane was leaving for California pretty soon, he said gently through the lavatory door. I told him I couldn't.

He started pounding on the door. Finally I had cleaned myself up as best I could and I rushed out of the plane.

My fellow stewardess had acted strangely since the beginning of the Syracuse flight. She was thin and blond, and looked like she was in her early 30's. She told me wild stories about how she was descended from royalty, how her family had villas all around the world, and how she was studying for her doctorate. She talked to herself as she walked up and down the aisle of the plane, and stood around smoking in the rear of the cabin. She was obviously suffering under a lot of tension.

Several of the other stewardesses I flew with during that first month on the Syracuse run also acted strangely. One women never took her coat off during the entire week that I flew with her. Another woman had been flying for eighteen months and was living in fear of death. During one particularly bumpy landing she grabbed my hand and whispered, "We're coming in too fast, we're going to crash." She squeezed my hand so hard that her nails left marks in my palm. I felt strange trying to be reassuring to a woman who had flown so much longer than I had.

Obviously being a stewardess was not quite the "impossible dream" our class had sung about. Most of the more experienced stewardesses seemed tired and strained, and this caused us all concern, because we knew we would be in their shoes in time.

But we still had that initial enthusiasm for the job, that romanticism about our own lives. We all wanted to be the best stewardesses there ever were. We figured we would find the romance and the adventure as soon as we had enough seniority to get good trips.

In June I was assigned a flight to five cities, with a layover in Syracuse, and then hopping from city to city back the following day. We flew in a little English jet that only seated sixty-six people, just a little two-engine compact that looked like a snub-nosed cigar.

There were two crew members and two stewardesses on the flight, and my costewardess, Judy, and I became the best of friends. We had a good time on those flights. It was like the theater, with the center aisle on the stage. It was a hectic schedule, with the average flying time being only about thirty minutes. You'd just go up and down, up and down all day and you could either go crazy or laugh at how terrible it was. We laughed and managed to give our passengers some frenzied humor.

The crew members dubbed us "The Dynamic Duo." They said they hadn't met such enthusiastic girls in a long time. We would plan pranks for them, like emptying their lunch boxes and filling them with garbage. And they would get their revenge. One evening in Syracuse the captain and copilot took us out to dinner and then to a bar, except they insisted that we both walk into the bar first, and then they ran off. It turned out to be a gay bar, and we stumbled back out into the street. The crew thought it was a hilarious joke.

That August I was assigned to fly to Mexico City, and that became the most romantic time of my flying career. I had a regular flight leaving Chicago in the morning and stopping off at St. Louis, Oklahoma City, Dallas, and getting into Mexico City around 9 P.M. The first time I flew into Mexico City we went to the hotel and once settled in our room, my stewardess friend pulled out her hair rollers, a sandwich, and a Coke and said, "Well, I'm set for the day." She said she didn't like to eat anything in Mexico, and was saving her money, so she just brought her food and read in her hotel room.

I couldn't believe it. Here was this beautiful, exotic city outside of our hotel windows. I called the other two stewardesses on the flight, and we went to a nightclub overlooking the city. The other women spoke fluent Spanish. Mine was only school Spanish, but I managed to carry on a conversation with some Mexican students who joined our table.

That month I experienced some of the glamor that is supposed to be the life of a stewardess. Glamor is a strange commodity, and you have to be in a particular state of mind to experience it.

We stayed in the best hotel in the city, and were treated

almost like movie stars by the Mexican men. We were wined and dined in a frantic night life.

I remember thinking, when one of my costewardesses was blond, of the sensation she would cause walking down the street in Mexico City. Blond hair and blue eyes have a big impact there because of their rarity. The men whistle and scream and jump up and down. We think hard hats react to women in this country, but in Mexico City they go wild.

I was living at a hectic pace, experiencing as much as I could during the evenings and mornings before the trips back to Chicago. My dreams were also at a frantic pace, with people talking to me in Spanish and English. There were a vast number of people in those dreams, hundreds of people, and I realized it must be because I was meeting so many thousands of people on the flights. Everything was going at a speeded up tempo, and I was trying to cram in as much as I could of Mexico City life.

I remember thinking that this was why I joined the airlines. I would even get angry with the other stewardesses if they stayed at the hotel and would not go out in the evenings, or join me in trips to the marketplace to bargain over prices.

There are levels of understanding of a place that come with time. Mexico City gets very cold at night, and a lot of people have migrated from the country to the outskirts of the city where they camp out, some living in shacks and some with less. They wear dark, coarsely woven wool clothing to protect themselves from the night. There were a lot of people begging on the streets.

I visited Acapulco several times, and it must be one of the most beautiful bays in the world. But each time I went, it seemed there was another fancy hotel, more poverty surrounding it, and more bitterness by the Mexicans, who would spit out *tourista* with hatred when they saw Americans drive by.

One day I took a bus to Toluca to see some of the life outside of Mexico City. There was a large outdoor marketplace in the square. The food was decomposing in the heat and flies were swarming around. Everybody seemed poor. I went into the church in the center of the plaza. There were ornate statues and a huge crucifix, with the blood pouring from Christ's side and the thorns tearing his head. I felt like I was in a totally alien world. I finally realized that visiting the Hilton Hotel was not living in Mexico.

I made friends with Edmundo, a student at the university. He was a tall, very dark Indian from a small town near Acapulco. He had studied for the priesthood, which he said was about the only way it was possible to get a secondary school education in the countryside. When we met he didn't speak any English, and I spoke very little Spanish, so we practiced our new language with each other.

Later that month there was a series of student demonstrations. The police mowed down students at the technical school with machine-gun fire. The government imposed censorship on the Mexican newspapers, and my friends and I brought American newspapers with us on each flight so that some of the students could try to keep up with events at their own university.

One day Edmundo said he was leaving the city. He said it was not a good time to be a student. Several of our other student friends also left town that same day.

The following month was the time of the Olympic games in Mexico City, and although I bid and got the flight, the glamor had disappeared. The flight had only a few hours stopover in Mexico City. The planes were jammed with people going to the games, and I began to wear down under the strain.

Even under the best of circumstances life would never seem so glamorous or exotic in Mexico City again.

The Flying Geisha Girls

THE former president of Pan American Airways, Najeeb Halaby, described what the airlines look for in stewardesses in a 1971 issue of the company's magazine. He told his stewardesses they should be more like Japanese geisha girls, prepared to flatter and entertain the male passengers.

There are some interesting parallels between the Japanese geisha and the airline stewardess. The geisha is impeccably dressed and coiffed. She is taught to move gracefully on her getas, or raised platform shoes. Her manners are carefully polished, and she is trained to be the perfect, charming, subservient hostess.

Geisha means a person of artistic talents, and the geisha is taught from early childhood to sing, recite, perform the tea ceremony, tickle customers, and whisper obscene jokes into a man's ear. But a geisha is never a prostitute. The customers must turn to courtesans for their more carnal needs. The geishas are organized much like trade unions, or guilds, and members usually serve under contract to a teahouse. The true geisha is trained by the guild from the time she is five or six to entertain and please men. That is her life.

The airlines' efforts to recreate a brassy version of the geisha in America have met with only mixed success. The advertising agencies have succeeded in creating the public image of the airline stewardess as a geisha girl. But the companies have had more difficulty convincing their stewardesses to play the role.

Madison Avenue agencies are most inspired when they are preparing campaigns for airlines from exotic lands. Japan Air Lines is, of course, a natural. The campaign promises "a lovely JAL hostess in kimono to introduce every passenger to the subtle delights of Japanese comfort and hospitality." China Airlines promises that you'll be "pampered by cheongsam-clad hostesses as you relax in an Oriental atmosphere." Air Jamaica stewardesses are referred to as "rare tropical birds."

It's hard to sound quite so exotic about American women. Subservient women from other cultures have long had a hold on American male sexual fantasies. But the American airlines do their best. Braniff had its "Air Strip." A few years ago TWA had its $1 million bonus, where mystery passengers handed sealed envelopes containing cash to award the stewardess of their choice at the end of the flight. Then there is the famous "Fly Me— I'm Cheryl" campaign by National Airlines.

This imagery has touched off an endless series of stewardess exploitation books, starting with *Coffee, Tea, or Me?,* now in its twentieth printing, and continuing down to the most recent entry, *How to Make a Good Stewardess,* which is not a "how-to" for stewardesses, but a purported guide as to the most effective means of seducing the different kinds of girls found on different airlines.

The airlines, of course, are not innocent victims of Madison Avenue. This was made clear during the controversy in early 1974 over the new slogan introduced by Continental Airlines:

"We really move our tails for you."

When stewardesses complained, a Continental official acknowledged to the press that the campaign was inspired by the 19 percent increase in passengers experienced by National Airlines after their "Fly Me" campaign.

Continental is offering its stewardesses a choice of snappy rejoinders to any remarks inspired by the campaign. A suggested answer to the question, "Will you move your tail for me?" is "Why, is it in the way?"

A second answer, offered on film to the stewardesses in the presentation of the campaign, is "You bet your ass." Continental also plans to hold a monthly contest for the best reply from an employee.

Regulated by the federal government on fares, the airlines remain determined to compete on the basis of service. The "service" mushroomed in the 1950's into a concerted effort to recruit, train, and supervise attractive, subservient women.

And they're still at it. A former personnel employee at

Pan American said, "Up until about a year ago, two guys did all the hiring, and we could always tell who hired whom. One went for the dark, exotic types, and the other went for the blond, remote queens." No one seriously disputes the fact that the airlines still hire on the basis of looks and personality, in that order.

Once you are on the job, your worth is judged by the company solely on the basis of the number of complimentary letters they get from satisfied customers (or, horror of horrors, letters of complaint), and occasional inflight inspections by your supervisor, who grades you on such things as "eye-to-eye contact" with customers and uniform appearance.

In fact, the evaluation system currently used by virtually all the lines would make a good report card for a geisha girl. The last time I was checked by my supervisor, on May 2, 1973, I was graded on the following items: eye-to-eye contact with customers during boarding and taxi-out, during food/beverage service, after food/ beverage service, and during taxi-in and deplaning. Also friendly facial expression, personalized transactions, and satisfactory closure on transactions during these four periods—a total of sixteen check marks on this item alone —which was entitled Customer Impact.

I received all "goods" except on friendly facial expression during boarding and taxi-out. The comment: "A friendly smile during phase one will help create a favorable impression." I didn't spot the supervisor until she was already on the plane or I would have grinned in phase one.

So this is the role the stewardess is expected to play—that seeming anomaly, an American geisha girl. The company, the crew, the passengers all tend to treat her accordingly, and, at least initially, she treats herself accordingly.

What does it feel like to play that role? Very few stewardesses who have been flying for more than a few years can stand that aspect of the job. We weren't trained since the age of six, after all, at least not quite so effectively trained.

I hate to think of the amount of motivational research that went into the airlines' calculations of how to procure and train obedient servants. One obvious finding must have been that you can only get it from eager beginners.

Some aspects of being an eager young geisha are aggravating and some just mildly amusing. I remember being given so many business cards during a day that my pockets would be bulging by the end of the flight. These businessmen, some that you hadn't even talked to, would come up at the end of the flight and hand you their card and say, "If you're ever in Tallahassee, look me up." We would nod and smile and stuff the card in our pockets along with the others. My roommates and I collected so many cards during the first month of flying that we finally threw them all into a big shopping bag—hundreds of engraved invitations.

Some men try to attract attention by grabbing an arm or a skirt, or tapping you on your behind. Their attitude seems to be that their ticket gives them the right to order the stewardess around. The worst passengers are the ones who take several drinks and then revert to childhood. They all seem to be convinced that the stewardess is just dying to hear their sexy little jokes. It got so that a man would just start telling a joke and I would walk away and have another stewardess wait on him from then on.

I came to feel that any sign of pleasantness or humanity would be misconstrued as a sexual come-on. It bothered me more and more, until finally I always expected the worst and avoided almost any direct contact with male passengers.

Jan Taylor had one of the most aggravating flights I've heard of. It happened last July on a trip from Philadelphia to Chicago, and trouble was obvious from the start. Three businessmen who were apparently returning from a golf outing and who were obviously a little tipsy boarded at Philadelphia, one of them managing to give Jan an intimate little pat as he went by.

They settled down in their seats, and started whistling and shouting for paper, pencils, and cards. They called Jan and the other stewardess "sweetheart" and "doll."

A large man dressed in bright purple slacks and green jersey took his seat in first class. He was apparently the boss of the men flying in coach. He called Jan over and told her, "You tell that little blond to have my friends come up here and sit." She replied that they would have to pay the difference in fare if they were going to travel first class. He argued for a while, but then the man sitting next to him asked for a deck of cards, and Jan went to get them.

During the meal service one of the men in coach demanded to visit with his friend in first class. When Jan told him he could not he looked at her with a condescending stare, turned, and strolled into the first-class section. She followed him and politely asked him to return to coach. He gave her a disgusted look and returned to coach, where he stood at his seat smoking a cigarette. Jan told him that there was an FAA regulation that you had to be seated to smoke.

"How long have you been flying?" he demanded to know. She replied that she had been flying four years, and that she did not make the rules. He handed his cigarette to a friend and remained standing, trying to stare her down each time she passed.

When the meal was almost over, the second man sitting in coach went to talk with the boss in first class. Jan followed him up the aisle, and stood behind him, tapping him on the shoulder. He pointedly ignored her. She said, "Sir, you will have to go back to the back cabin." He replied, "I will in a minute."

Meanwhile the boss, who had consumed a bourbon and a Manhattan and was slurring his words, said something laughingly and reached out to grab at the second friend's crotch, missing him as the friend jumped back. They were both laughing.

Then the boss swung his arm out and grabbed at Jan's crotch, not missing her. She grabbed his hand, slapped it hard, and shouted angrily, "Get your hand off me." It was a reflex action, and in that instant all pretense of politeness left her. They all stood there for a moment, shocked.

The boss mumbled that he was sorry, that he hadn't

known it was Jan standing there, that he had thought it was another friend. Jan told the second friend to please return to the back cabin. He replied once again, "In just a minute."

Jan returned to the aft galley, trying to control her rage. A few minutes later she saw that the second friend was still there, standing and conversing with the boss. Jan went up to them once more, and said that if he did not return to his seat she would call the captain. "Get him then," he replied.

Jan broke down and cried in relating the story to the captain. The captain came forward and in a friendly manner asked the men to kindly keep their hands off the stewardesses and warned that if there was any more trouble he would call the cops in Chicago. But he said it in such a friendly way that he clearly sympathized with the men.

Jan sat in the galley for the rest of the flight, trying to release the tension that had accumulated from holding her anger and humiliation under control by crying. She decided that she would feel less humiliated if she expressed herself to these men as an equal.

As the plane taxied in, she stepped into the cabin and asked the three men, "Are any of you at all sorry for anything that's gone on here?"

When two of them gave a resounding "no!" she said, "Then I would just like you to know what pitiful and disgusting people I think you and your friend up front are." They were shocked. They were incensed. They demanded to know her name so they could complain to the company. She asked for theirs so she could inform their company how they had behaved. Finally one of them said, "Look, I'll apologize for the three of us even though I don't think we did anything to apologize for. We didn't mean to be disrespectful."

Jan replied, "That's the sad part about it. You people never mean to be disrespectful, yet we take your abuse day after day."

You could say that the main problem on that flight was that drunken passengers were allowed on board, which they are not supposed to be. Or that too much liquor is served on flights and should be limited or cut out altogether.

But the deeper problem is the basic lack of respect for the stewardess. She is, after all, the person in charge of passenger safety. She is responsible for activity in the passenger section of the plane. If there is a crash, passengers' lives will depend on her ability and her courage. But her image is not conducive to being able to exercise authority.

Geishas do not have authority. Geishas gladly serve.

And it's not only the passengers who are caught up in the imagery and tend to treat stewardesses accordingly. Flight crews, company management, even husbands and boyfriends tend to treat us in stereotyped ways.

Several of my friends have dated men who said they wished they'd met them on a flight. They felt that would be very romantic. A friend who flies with United had a boyfriend who became entranced with the idea of her role. Finally he arranged to fly from New York to Los

Angeles on one of her flights, and years later he was still talking about their cross-country romance.

"It was the greatest service I ever had," he would brag. It doesn't take a sociologist to see that he was caught up in the fantasy of being served hand and foot.

Worst of all are some of the flight crews. There are many pilots and navigators who are the finest and most sensitive of people. But pilots have a tendency to see themselves in an allegorical role. They are the men in charge of the ship.

In fact, they tend to see the plane as a metaphor for the ideal roles between men and women; the captain the boss, the stewardess his obedient servant. Which is why they tend to be the most upset by some of the changes that are going on in the airline industry today.

A group of pilots was recently reminiscing about the good old days before there were any male flight attendants at Chicago's O'Hare Airport. One pilot mused, "For a while there you had to knock on the stewardesses' doors. Then," he continued, "it got to the point where they'd knock on our doors. But now, these guys (meaning the recently introduced male flight attendants) are getting all the action."

Most of that speech is bluster, but it does have some symbolic meaning. The fifteen pilots sitting around that table all nodded sagely in agreement. There's no question that the recent advent of male flight attendants has challenged many a pilot's concept of his masculinity.

There is very little carrying on between pilots and

stewardesses these days. One captain said that stewardesses were so angry with the stereotyped relations between stewardesses and crew that they "just won't have
anything to do with us." But some crews still take the
attitude that beginning stewardesses have an obligation
to go out with them.

Anna had a hard time fending off a pilot one night
during a layover in Kansas City. The pilot and copilot
came up to the room she was sharing with her costewardess, bringing along a couple of bottles of cold duck. They
all chatted for a while, and then Anna said she was really
tired and was going to turn in.

She went into the bathroom and was taking a shower
when she felt someone touching the shower curtain. She
held onto it in a panic. The naked man's leg appeared
through the side of the curtain.

She suddenly lost her fear and got angry. She yelled at
him, "You get away from here or I'll see that you lose
your job," and the pilot hurriedly got dressed and beat a
retreat. The next morning she learned that he had been
knocking on another stewardess' door later that night
trying to get in.

The attitude of the top management of the airlines is
not reassuring in these matters. Last winter a stewardess
was raped by a pilot in Chicago and the company, one of
the major domestic airlines, refused to take any action
against the pilot. In one of the preliminary negotiations
on the matter, a man representing the stewardess was told
by a top management official who knew nothing about

the case: "You've got to remember, these girls provoke this sort of thing."

Finally the pilot was disciplined—for drinking within a twenty-four-hour restriction before a flight, not for his sexual attack.

All this is not to say that all businessmen are drunken, insensitive slobs or that all pilots are sex-crazed monsters. But there's no question that the public image of the stewardess as a geisha girl leads to these kinds of problems.

As long as we try to play the role—smiling constantly at every passenger, making eye contact with each, trying to please by the way we dress and make ourselves up and walk and serve a passenger's needs—we are the counterpart of the geisha.

And as successful as we become in adopting that role, just that much do we lose in maintaining our personal identity, our own ego, our own will. We become automatons, windup Barbie dolls, invisible people.

Japanese journalist Aisaburo Akiyama wrote a booklet on the geisha in the 1920's. He concluded, "Geisha girls are almost forced, as it were, to commit spiritual suicide, so that it is but natural they abandon themselves to desperation, eventually making themselves like a rudderless boat floating on the wild ocean."

Airline stewardesses have not been trained since childhood. They do not suffer the total subjugation of the geisha. But anyone who has been a stewardess will understand at a very deep level the phenomenon he was describing.

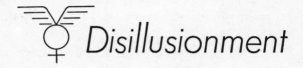 *Disillusionment*

AT some point in the career of almost every stewardess there comes a moment of total disillusionment. It usually happens toward the latter half of your first year of flying, triggered by some minor problem. But suddenly all the destructive and humiliating experiences of flying well up inside you, and in a moment of clarity you see the shabby reality through the remnants of the dream.

I went through a series of experiences at the end of my first year that were out of keeping with my concept of what the job was all about. Any vestiges of the myths that had been fed into us during the training school were erased, and I began to see what was really happening around me.

The moment that it hit me the hardest was in the middle of this bleak period, on a flight from God knows where back to Chicago. I had been on standby all month, and was totally disoriented as to whether it was day or night. There had been severe turbulences on the flight; the plane had been hitting air currents, causing it to lurch from side to side and up and down at the same time. I got sick to my stomach and there was coffee spilled all over my apron. My uniform was a mess.

I looked at myself in the mirror and saw a stranger. That wasn't who I was. Not that disheveled girl with the pale, sickly skin and the vacant dull eyes. It looked like somebody else.

The next day I didn't want to put my uniform on, and when I finally forced myself to, I felt worthless, an object, a robot that wasn't supposed to have a brain. I looked at myself in the mirror again and I saw just a body detached from my mind.

I had graduated. I had become an experienced stewardess.

The depth of anger that we develop toward the company was probably most dramatically expressed by TWA stewardess Catherine Culver, who was involved in a hijack attempt in June 1971. The hijacker forced his way on board at Chicago's O'Hare International Airport. He did not have a boarding pass, and Catherine asked him to leave. He pulled a pistol out of an umbrella he was carrying, grabbed her around the neck, and held the gun to her head.

The passengers began scrambling off the plane, when one of them, a sixty-five-year-old management consultant from Darien, Connecticut, lunged at the hijacker, and was shot in the chest. The wounded man began crawling to safety, was shot again in the back, and died. The hijacker allowed airline workers to remove the body, and then insisted on flying to North Vietnam.

"I tried to calm him down," Catherine recalled when I interviewed her. "We talked, and I held his hand, but it was difficult. Hijackers are suicidal."

After about thirty minutes in the air, he left her and walked toward the front of the plane, and a marshall that had been smuggled through a window of the cockpit during the delay at O'Hare opened fire on him.

There was an exchange of six shots back and forth, while Catherine lay on the floor underneath a seat in the middle of the cabin. Then for the remainder of the flight everyone lay on the floor, without a word said. When they landed in New York there was another exchange of shots and the wounded hijacker was arrested.

"Even when I was under that seat, the bullets going over my head, I was thinking about the company," Catherine said. "I was thinking 'they'll just scratch my name off the list, and replace me with someone else. My parents will probably have to pay for a pass to come and get my body.'"

Catherine also resented the way the newpapers described the fact that after she had been up for thirty-two hours straight, she was interviewed in Chicago. Two days after the incident she broke down.

"I started crying at the end of the interview and there were all these pictures in the paper of me wiping away a tear. They really pounced on that."

Only one woman passenger was quoted in the newspaper account as commenting on the fact that Catherine had been courageous—that with a gun to her head, a dead man lying at her feet, she had maintained control, had instructed passengers to leave the plane, had engaged the hijacker in conversation.

She was given a week off by the company, but at a lower pay rate than if she had been flying. Then she became just another number. The company hates to draw attention to a hijacking. Company officials tried to pretend it had never happened.

For most of us the disillusionment is not so dramatic, but it goes just as deep.

The winter of my disillusionment was very cold, and it would take as much as two hours to get to the airport through the snow. I was flying standby, and would have to sit for hours in my apartment, waiting for the phone to ring to be summoned for a flight. You can't plan to do anything because you have to be ready at a moment's notice, immaculately dressed and groomed. You aren't even allowed to wash your hair, because you might not be ready to go when called.

I would sit there at a conscious level before fantasy, in a total withdrawal into self, almost like a catatonic. I didn't want to do anything because I might get myself dirty. I would just wait, for hours or for days, for the phone to ring. I had never taken any drugs at the time, but the state of mind was very much like when I had surgery the following month and was given Demerol for the pain—a feeling of floating in the unconscious. I don't know anybody, even the most experienced flyers, who don't experience some terror when they are on standby.

Christmas is the most difficult time for the airlines. Every flight is scheduled to be full, and when weather conditions force cancellations, there are long delays, uncertain flight times, forced landings in other cities, Christmas packages crowding the planes that shouldn't be allowed on board, and drunken passengers.

One day in mid-December I got to the airport and was signing in for my flight when the crew scheduler received a phone call and said, "Quick, there's a flight leaving in five minutes for L. A. and they're one girl short. You can come back tonight."

So I rushed along the K concourse and boarded the L.A. flight. When we arrived the crew scheduler there said it was a three-day trip and I would have to finish it with the other stewardesses. So I flew for the three days. Then it snowed and we got stuck in New York on the third day. They sent the other three women home to L.A., and put me on a two-day flight to the Southwest.

Meanwhile the office in Chicago called my parents in Massachusetts and told them I was missing. My mother was stunned.

If a stewardess is missing for three days she is considered to have quit, so there was a lot of straightening out to do when I finally got back to Chicago. I learned never to be so blindly obedient to a crew scheduler again.

The next month I had a nightmare flight that made me wonder about the humanity of human beings. It was a long flight from Mexico City, and I was serving in first class where the liquor was free. Some of the passengers had been drinking cocktails, wine, and champagne with their meals, and liqueurs afterwards.

Suddenly an elderly woman in an aisle seat grasped her chest and said she had a terrible pain. She was pale. I checked her lips and fingers and they had a blue tinge that indicated a lack of oxygen.

She said she had had some heart trouble and had recently been in the hospital. I laid her down in the aisle, got an oxygen tank, and administered the oxygen to her.

As I was leaning over her I told the other stewardess to make sure that cigarettes were put out nearby. It's a federal rule that you have to extinguish cigarettes in the three rows around where you are giving oxygen because a spark could touch off a fire. But one woman refused to put out her cigarette.

She started yelling, "I paid for this seat and I'm going to smoke this cigarette." I told the other stewardess to get her out of there and up to the jump seat at the front of the plane. She managed to do it, the woman drunkenly shouting and cursing the while.

Then the passenger sitting next to my head (because I was on the floor in the aisle, bending over the stricken woman) began to bang his coffee cup on the side of the chair, demanding more coffee.

He was looking right at me as I was administering the oxygen, banging that cup in my ear and demanding more coffee immediately. I couldn't believe it. I absolutely could not believe that anyone could be so devoid of humanity that he could think his cup of coffee was more important than the health of someone who might be dying.

Meanwhile the cigarette-smoking woman was standing up front, screaming about how bad the company was, not letting her have a cigarette. She and the man were obviously drunk.

An ambulance was waiting for the stricken woman when we landed in Chicago, and an agent told me she appeared to be all right when they drove her away.

I fell into a real depression after that. I had trouble sleeping at night, and would stay up reading into the morning hours. I would walk around the quiet apartment, wondering what I was doing with my life. Then I had a terrible time waking up; I would sleep until noon or one o'clock. I had trouble starting and then once I got started I had trouble stopping.

My state of mind was such that I felt I was just nothing behind the stewardess uniform. That I was a waitress, serving passengers. That I was supposed to serve, and be nothing. My spirit was broken. I would go along with whatever they said.

One morning my mother called and said my father had just gone to the hospital. I had not been home in the ten months I'd been flying, and my father being sick troubled me. I went to medical to try to get a few days off for sick leave to fly back to see him. I had a terrible cold.

The doctor examined me and then sat back behind his desk, a short thin man with a large nose. He told me the only thing wrong with me was that I was sexually frustrated. "What you need is a good lay," he said. "I've been around stewardesses for years and I know what kind of things go wrong." I was really incensed by his attitude, but I didn't know what I could do about it. Eventually, I did manage to get a few days off, and I flew home. By the time I got to Brockton I had the flu so bad my mother insisted I see a doctor, and I reported in that I had to stretch the leave to four days.

When I got back to Chicago I was reprimanded. There were something like 160 of the 750 stewardesses on the line out with the flu, and we were all reprimanded. They were accusing us all of feigning illness during the Christmas rush.

I decided right then that the company just didn't care about us at all, was only using us, pushing us. We were always guilty unless proven innocent, and there was always that shadow of self-doubt that we would feel because the company distrusted us.

The following months recede into a blur of sameness. It was a time of constant travel, of being expected to act like a wind-up watch, of living a myth that I no longer believed in. There was slight compensation in the thought that other people still believed in the myth, and assumed I must be leading a romantic, glamorous life. But it was slight compensation indeed.

What do you do? I am an airline stewardess. Didn't you notice the uniform? Don't you know this is a stewardess hotel? Up at 4 A.M. in Rochester to travel to the airport, charged for tardiness if you are not an hour early for the flight, no matter what the reason. Ten cities in two days. Waking up screaming and sweating in a nightmarish yellow world. Where am I? What time is it? Is it 9 in the day or night? Is that New York time or Chicago time? Slowly establishing contact with reality and, still perspiring nervously, finding out that it is only a yellow hotel room in Mexico City and that it is nine o'clock in the evening.

You can finally reach a state of rootlessness and loss of identity that one of my friends describes as anomie—a feeling of total alienation from society, of being alone, unrelated to any community or any values.

I got married during my second year of flying, and tried to become basically a wife. When I wasn't flying I tried to dissociate it from my real life. I never mentioned the fact that I was a stewardess to my husband's friends. I bid only for the short trips, so that I would be home again the same day. I started building a wall around myself.

There were some advantages to the job. I now had free passes and my husband and I would fly to Acapulco or Los Angeles for the weekend. I figured that probably just about all jobs were miserable, and that at least this one had some good fringe benefits.

But even within this context it bore down on me. I started taking leaves and rebelling in small ways. If my supervisor chewed me out in front of other people, I would tell her that I would see her privately, and walk away. I was of course always accused of insubordination.

There is a rule that you are supposed to sign in one

hour before flight time, and if you are seven minutes late, they will call in a woman who is on reserve.

I would always arrive at the airport on time, and then have a cup of coffee and wait until the last possible moment to sign in—sometimes at six minutes and fifty-nine seconds into the hour's grace period.

I would play games of noncomformity with the airline. I refused to wear my name tag, and would tell my supervisor that I couldn't find it, or whatever. Once I was told that my navy uniform shoes weren't regulation because they had a one-half-inch platform sole. So to be belligerent I wore black crepe-soled shoes that were very comfortable, even if nonregulation.

After that first year I almost never wore my name tag. I didn't want people to know my name. It gave me some anonymity. My supervisors were always ordering new ones for me since I would have to give the excuse that it was lost.

By the end of my flying career my rebellion had really gotten out of hand. There is a saying among stewardesses that a pilot gains his identity by putting on his uniform, and a stewardess loses hers. My uniform was two sizes too big for me during those last few flights. My friends would tease me, but I really enjoyed swimming around in my sexless baggy dress.

I wasn't any too charming either. I just wouldn't smile all the time, like you were supposed to. I would tell my supervisor that only morons smile all the time. I was regularly reprimanded for my somber expression, but when our supervisors rode in the cabin to evaluate our performance I would usually spot them in time and smile my way through that one flight.

During my last year I would regularly get sick when it was time to fly. I would become nauseated, would have to vomit, and would get terrible stomach cramps. My doctor said it was apparently psychosomatic. My body was in open revolt against my life.

During the last month of flying, in June of 1973, I managed to have some fun with a fellow stewardess on a flight to and from Los Angeles. We played a game called "female chauvinism." The two of us would walk down the aisle, chatting intently to each other, and carefully examining the male passengers.

"Do you like this one?" I would ask, indicating a blond student. "How about him?" she would reply, nodding her head toward a respectable-looking businessman.

But the game had some unexpected results. We were trying to dehumanize these men by considering them sex objects, but they thought we were serious. They were also invariably very curious and very flattered. Role reversals can be tricky business.

I finally decided one day that I just didn't have to do this any more. A lot of stewardesses suffer from a deep insecurity, a feeling that if they weren't flying, they wouldn't be good enough for anything else. I shared that fear, but I finally worked up the courage to feel that certainly I could do something more worthwhile.

I did not formally announce my retirement. If you do, there is usually a formal kind of ceremony on your last flight. You wear your flight wings upside down, and everyone on the crew makes a spectacle of the whole thing. I certainly didn't want that. I just wanted to quit, so I called up and said, "I quit."

I don't think I have ever felt a greater jubilation, a greater feeling of well being, than the day I quit. My husband and I celebrated late into the night.

I was still unsure of my identity. I wasn't sure what I was going to do with my life, beyond taking more courses at the University of Illinois. But one thing I did know with finality. I was no longer an airline stewardess. I would never have to put that uniform on again.

I began to work on this book shortly before I quit, and at that time I was angry about what had happened to me during my years of flying. I was bent on destroying the myth of the stewardess as a carefree and glamorous sex symbol. But as the book progressed, and I started working with several stewardess organizations and an investigative reporter, the reasons for the creation of the myth became apparent, and the disastrous effects it had on all flight attendants became clear.

Because they regard us as fluffy publicity-getters, as marketable sex objects, the airlines have exposed us to needless health and safety hazards; have, in fact, forgotten that we are human beings. In their efforts to increase their sales, the airlines have taken careless chances with the health and safety of stewardesses and passengers alike.

The Neurotic Companies

WHEN I first started flying I couldn't help but notice the stress that several of the older stewardesses were suffering. The stewardess who shoveled food over my head when my finger was caught or the one who panicked at the idea of a plane crash—they were all what would normally be considered neurotic people.

A few years later, when I was scowling, adamant about my rights under the contract, psychosomatically sick before flights, I must have struck many young stewardesses in the same way.

What happens? What transforms a young stewardess, eager to please, into a growling, bitter neurotic? What is there about the job that makes the rate of stewardesses receiving psychiatric care so high?

The companies' pat explanation for the problems that stewardesses suffer is that they are somehow the fault of the stewardesses themselves, and either the selection process should be changed to find less neurotic women, or the schooling and counseling should be modified to better maintain stewardesses on the job.

Whatever the rationalization, everyone connected with the airline industry is familiar with the phenomena. *Five Million Miles,* a boosterish book about the history of the airlines published in 1965, observes: "As the years go by, unless she watches herself, a stewardess can build up a deep and permanent resentment against people in general." Later on in the book the author puzzles over the fact that stewardesses on some foreign airlines do not seem to deteriorate in the same kind of way.

In 1967, American Airlines tried to use this phenomenon as the basis for defending its policy of forcing women to stop flying at thirty-two. "Senior stewardesses may experience emotional problems resulting from the absence of a permanent home and family relationship," read the airline's statement submitted to a House Sub-Committee investigating age discrimination. Since the airline at the time did not permit marriage or children, which presumably would constitute the "permanent home and family relationship," it is a wonderful example of circular reasoning.

More recently, the airlines have focused more energies on the recruiting stage, realizing that growing tenure and job security are making the "neurotic" stewardess a more lasting problem. The psychologist for a major airline was quoted recently as indicating that the problem was caused by the recruitment of neurotic women.

"It's about time the airlines gave their recruiting standards a close look," he said. "The emphasis, no matter what the official line is, rests squarely on looks first and a vaguely construed conception of the 'giving personality' second. But what I'm seeing more often than I like is a bunch of neurotics who need to serve rather than those who want to serve. She's the ex-prom queen who craves the mass admiration she got the night she was crowned, or the girl who never could please daddy. That poor kid is flying around trying to please hundreds of daddies. Both types have weak ego structures and both get bitchy when they find out what the job really entails. But the important point I'm trying to make is that this personality type is disastrous for the airline and for the flying public. She's not really giving at all. She's taking."

This seems to be a call for reform, but note that the entire problem rests with the stewardesses who were chosen, not with the job itself, or with what the advertising and public relations departments have done to that job. Notice the resentment expressed against the "bitchy" stewardess, the "bunch of neurotics," the stewardess who is "taking."

There is certainly truth to the charge that the airlines use the wrong kind of criteria in selecting stewardesses. But that does not mean that you can blame the victim for the crime. There is good reason to believe that no matter who was selected, they would suffer much the same kind of mental stress.

David Roadhouse, a psychiatric counselor who has treated a number of stewardesses, has come to the conclusion that it is the airlines themselves who are neurotic.

I was referred to him by the Stewardesses For Women's Rights, and that first interview in his downtown Chicago office was a revelation to me. I had always believed the company's line about stewardesses not measuring up to expectations. I was not a patient, and Roadhouse was not dealing with my personal problems, but I emerged from that interview elated, my world view reeling.

"The script that airline stewardesses are supposed to play is a neurotic one," he said. "They cast the young American female as a picture book sex object. She's around to appeal to all."

He said there was nothing wrong with a job that involved helping people be comfortable and alerting them to safety. What was wrong was the gap between the job function and the role created by the airlines to fulfill that function.

"The airlines are insecure. They fear that if they gave more freedom to stewardesses about what they wear and how they conduct themselves with the passengers they might lose money. They fear losing control over the stewardesses.

"Stewardesses are the only airline employees who are checked on uniform and appearance. There are regulations for other airline employees, but no checks. It's like the quality control department in an industrial plant. The procedure is really sick, and in no way supports a woman's health-producing, maturing mechanism.

"Mommy, the supervisor, knows what daddy, the corporate boss, wants."

The only thing that keeps a woman playing the role is a pessimism about her own personal development, he said. She feels that all she has to offer is to perfect a script that someone else has written for her.

I remember my small acts of rebellion against the company and asked him if that was a sign I was ready to break into the real world. He said that kind of rebellion did mark the beginning of personal development.

"Rebellion is the beginning of a resolution," he said, "much like an adolescent rebellion is the beginning of a resolution of personal identity."

I told him about the depression that I had suffered when I first started working on the book, how I had felt terrible for days after spending an evening going over why I became a stewardess and what I was like when I first started flying.

Roadhouse considered this depression a healthy thing, too. He said that any change and development in our concept of ourselves is accompanied by the pain of losing our former identity.

He said that the romanticization of flying was very much like the romance of the Marine Corps. The Marine is an upright, clean, loyal, polite, attentive male with a minimal amount of personal reactions.

There is a special romance associated with flying because it is so transient and there is a minimal amount of attachments that can occur. "This lends itself to a romanticism that is not unlike the honeymoon phase of a couple's relationship," he said, "the initial phase when everything is new."

But when the honeymoon is over a lot of stewardesses hang on and "then the romance with the romantic comes out. Stewardesses realize that everyone else thinks what they are doing is romantic. They realize that they don't feel that way anymore, and this is the first realization they have of the script they are playing. But the romance with the romantic has to last to a certain extent in order for the stewardess to stay on."

I asked him what he thought could be done to change the impossible script and make the job more bearable.

"The airline bosses can't change it," he said. "Only stewardesses can, to the extent they claim what is theirs. They can demand change and teach the airline officials they don't have to be so paranoid and controlling."

The interview with Roadhouse was a revelation for me. It was the first time I was supported, that some outside authority had at least abstractly backed up the feelings shared by me and most of my stewardess friends. It wasn't we who were crazy, it was the airlines.

So many things that I had felt guilty about for so long —guilty because I was an employee taking the company's money and not doing anything expected of me, guilty because of my acts of rebellion—were wiped away. Someone had backed us up in our belief that it was a sick job, a world turned inside out.

I've always had more personal strength since that day. I had gone to a psychiatrist briefly during my fifth year of flying, and he had just sat there and listened, and finally I stopped going. Roadhouse did more for me in one interview than all those official psychiatric sessions.

Over the following weeks and months I was able to slowly piece my life back together. Things that I had blacked out started coming back to me.

I remembered that it was after the company PR man clutched my head and stroked my face on that flight to Mexico that I had to take a three-month leave of absence. That was an expression of the pent-up rage within me.

I remembered how I became psychosomatically sick after that three-month period every time I got on a plane. I went back to work in December, and I would be sick to my stomach on most flights.

I was sick from January through March, always when it was time to take a flight, and the doctors couldn't tell me what was the matter. It was now so clear that my whole being was rebelling against the job.

But I didn't fully realize that. I went back to flying in April and May, and finally quit in June. I didn't even go to a psychiatrist until May, and that was no help.

I didn't rationally decide to quit. On the last flight I was supposed to take I just couldn't get on the plane.

The Roadhouse theory helps interpret a lot of the things that happen on the airlines. The efforts of the company's house psychologists to put a new veneer on the status quo look like the rationalizations they are.

I remember the time the company required everyone to report to the O'Hare hangar on an assigned day for a long session on the techniques of *I'm OK, You're OK.*

There's nothing wrong with the theory. There are three basic responses, the theory has it, of parent, adult, and child. The parental response is heavy-handed and stern. The adult response is mature and reasonable. The childish response is emotional.

We were given a presentation with slides and workshops with the idea of being able to apply some of this theory to passengers. We were supposed to be adult at all times, and to realize that when someone said, "this is a lousy airplane" or "stewardesses are whores," he was just being parental, and when he said, "Why are you giving me cold food?" or "What have you got against me?" he was being a child. We were supposed to learn how to bring the adult out.

The theory worked fine, but the workshop was a disaster, and the technique didn't seem to help. But the Roadhouse hypothesis explains why. The workshops didn't work because the supervisors who led them always played a parental role. And the technique was less than effective on board the plane because passengers automatically related to us, not as adults, but as children, as fluffy young things.

You have to attack the problems on board an airplane at a deeper level than that.

The
Stewardess Revolt

A FEMINIST revolt began sweeping through the airline industry in the 1970's. You could see it in a new mood of militancy in the stewardess unions, in the formation of ad hoc groups of stewardesses banding together to protect their rights, and even among some of the women who have been promoted to management positions.

At the center of the storm is a new organization called Stewardesses For Womens Rights. The group held its second national conference in Chicago in the fall of 1973. Plans were announced to file a broad lawsuit against one of the airlines charging discrimination against women in such matters as weight restrictions, promotional opportunities, and hiring practices.

The conference was my first extended contact with SFWR, and it was an invigorating experience to join so many concerned stewardesses who felt the way I did and were doing something about it. I realized my personal feelings were part of a general rebellion, and I met

84

women who had been struggling for years with the problems that I had just begun to recognize a few months before.

I admired these women, because it is rare enough for people to get involved in labor struggles or political struggles of any kind. It involves a shift in your attitude toward yourself and your job. And in this group there was the additional commitment to women's rights, which sets you even further outside the traditional wisdom, and forces you to redefine your entire life.

One evening session, devoted to a discussion of "Our Psychological State," was particularly interesting because it was an effort by the group to work its way through many of the political and personal problems that are confronting all women. The give and take of that session showed the process by which the SFWR women come to understand the problems that are common to all stewardesses.

The session was held in a lounge at Saint Chrysostom's Church on Chicago's North Side. Some fifty women, ranging in age from twenty to thirty-five, almost all of them active stewardesses, were seated around the lectern. The guest speaker was David Roadhouse, the psychiatric counsellor I had interviewed a few days before.

"The airlines have written a script for their flight attendants," he began; "a script meant to market them in order to get more passengers on their planes. The script calls for you to be polite, sexy, and seductive for the passengers. You are being asked to perform a role, and it is a dehumanizing, depersonalizing role. A lot of feelings go on inside you, but outside you are expected to always be polite, charming, and seductive for the passengers. But, increasingly, I am running across the phenomenon of women saying they don't have to market themselves for a corporation."

His remarks set off a series of responses from the stewardesses.

"Passengers ask me a personal question, like how tall I am," one relates. "I tell them, 'I'm sorry, but it's not part of my job to tell you that kind of thing.'"

"When passengers give me a hard time," another woman joins in, "I tell them, 'Your ticket does not give you the right to be abusive.'"

"You can't be passive," said a third. "That way you will only sit there and fume, and then it will come out inappropriately somewhere else."

Then Paula Neilson, a stewardess from Kansas City, described what it "does to your head" when you play out the company script.

"It used to be that I couldn't go on an airplane without my false eyelashes and hairpiece," she said. "It was a way of putting down other women. I knew I looked as good as anyone on the plane."

"Then I began to think, 'somebody is making money off of us.' I was telling myself that I was simply meeting my own standards; but then I realized that in fact they were forcing sisters to compete. When we do 'gussy' ourselves up on an airplane, we are saying, 'the only thing they are going to judge me on is my looks.' But when we don't do it, we're insecure. It's a dilemma."

A woman wearing blue jeans, a blouse, and no makeup, sitting on a couch over on the far side of the room, interjected: "Do you think men as a whole are better looking than women? Of course not. So why should we have to doll ourselves up? I never wear makeup on the plane."

There was a lot of disagreement on this issue until Jan Taylor, the chairperson for the conference, said that questions of appearance were a personal thing, and what we were discussing was the efforts by the airlines to force us into a single mold.

Roadhouse touched on some of the reasons why women become stewardesses.

"One of the reasons women join is to keep things happening, to keep moving all the time. It fits in with a whole flighty personality, where you don't have to deal with people. That does not mean to say that to be an airline stewardess is to be neurotic."

But several stewardesses disagreed.

"I think it's just the opposite of escapism," said one. "When you walk on that plane, you have to try to work up an instant rapport with a whole planeload of people. Sometimes it works, and it's a far out trip. Sometimes it doesn't."

"It's a lot like being a stage actress," said another. "You have to try to set up that immediate rapport with an audience, and you have to enjoy it, like an actress. A lot of people—salespeople, politicians—meet a lot of people and don't get to know them well, but that doesn't mean they are all neurotic, that they don't have permanent, deep relationships."

Jan Taylor added: "One of the hardest things to realize is how much we are really not ourselves. One of the things each of us can do is to try to implement more of ourselves, express more of our personal feelings."

"Just in the past five years," another stewardess added, "women have become more in touch with themselves. Women are just finding a new identity."

There was general agreement on that, and the meeting moved to a discussion among friends of what it was like to be searching for one's identity in a culture that stereotypes women. Someone described a typical reaction by a stewardess to the SFWR: "Is that one of those groups where you sit around and call each other sister?"

I asked what the feelings were about the recent trend toward more sexy uniforms, hot pants, and strip shows on airplanes. I remarked that as far as I could see, stewardesses on the major airlines had much more conservative and professional looking uniforms until Braniff International came along with the couture outfits and strip shows in 1965, and the other airlines followed suit in the late 1960's.

"We used to have somewhat military uniforms," said Elizabeth Rich, a distinguished looking young woman who is the SFWR historian and the author of several books on the airlines. "It used to be more of a Doris Day kind of thing. We were a sweetheart then, not a sex symbol. Sex was a more covert thing in those days." Karen Eitelberg also thought the stewardess profession had lost a lot in the transition.

"I would like to get back to a very classic, perhaps even paramilitary uniform instead of the hot pants kind of thing," she said. "When I taught school I always wore something that made me feel proud. I would look in the mirror and see a professional, competent person. A more dignified uniform would help us have the authority we need to do our job."

There seemed to be virtually unanimous agreement that a more professional-looking uniform would help to restore some of the pride in the profession. One woman noted that the new male stewards have more military-looking uniforms, and a second suggested that the airline's new emphasis on youthfulness and sexiness might be related to their efforts to force more experienced stewardesses to quit. After all, a thirty-five-year-old woman feels pretty silly if she has to wear hot pants.

Sandra Jarrell, the founder of SFWR, described the difficulties that we have all been confronted with in trying to shift from the role of stewardess to activist. A quiet women in her mid-twenties, with brown hair and a brown dress, she spoke forcefully.

"I think we all tend to have an undeveloped logical, aggressive side to our personalities," she said. "It's so underdeveloped that the people heading the organization suffer from it. We have to combat the feeling that we are helpless, that the situation is hopeless, that we can't do anything about it.

"A long time ago we just didn't learn to deal with certain kinds of problems. Now we are having to learn how to deal with the laws, how to bring about change. There is so much to do. My involvement in this organization has been the hardest thing that ever happened to me.

"But that first step, deciding that you want to do it, that there are actions that have to be taken—was the greatest feeling I've ever had."

Several other women described that feeling of jubilation that had come over them when they finally decided that they no longer were going to suffer passively, but were going to struggle to bring about change. They also described the feelings of isolation and loneliness that come when you can't communicate your new feelings to even some of your closest friends, when you are written off as a "women's libber." But there was also a shared feeling of commitment to an important cause, and a conviction that SFWR is working to discard the old, dehumanizing sex roles and helping to create new women and, eventually, new men.

Sandra Jarrell was a stewardess for Eastern Airlines for three years, quitting at the end of 1971 after a long series of frustrating run-ins with the company on petty regulations.

"No matter how well I performed my job, I would be judged only on the silliest, inconsequential matters," Ms. Jarrell said. After leaving the airline she brooded for a month, and then decided that someone had to do something to change the exploitation of women as stewardesses.

She and Jan Fulsom, another Eastern stewardess who had just quit, decided to try to organize. They prepared a mimeographed newsletter and sent it to 320 Eastern stewardesses, explaining that there was a small group forming to try to change the image of flight attendants.

Some of the letters were taken out of the mailboxes and sent back to the post office, so the two organizers went to Washington National Airport and distributed the leaflets themselves. Only about twenty stewardesses came to that first organizational meeting in the National Press Building in Washington, but that was enough to launch the new organization.

The group held a press conference in February of 1972, and the resulting publicity led to an unexpected outpouring of response. SFWR received an average of 150 letters and seventy-five phone calls a week from stewardesses and concerned women from all over the country who wanted to find out more about their efforts or to join in the struggle.

SFWR developed a basic statement of purpose which was printed in their newsletter: "Women of all races are underutilized in the airline industry," it read, "relegated to low paying jobs, or assigned to public service roles where they are stigmatized as sex objects. The position that overtly reflects this lack of opportunity for advancement is that of stewardess. Airlines have exploited their personnel through advertising ('I'm Cheryl, Fly Me' campaign) and through other shoddy and suggestive campaigns which depict the stewardess as an empty-headed Barbie doll.

"The airlines refuse as a whole to acknowledge the fact that stewardesses are required by federal law to be on board airplanes—as stated in Federal Aviation Regulation 121.391, 'to provide the most effective egress of passengers in the event of an emergency evacuation.' Airlines have responded apathetically to women's needs and to the growing reevaluation of women's roles in society. They continue to perpetuate an outdated value system rather than provide a sincere atmosphere for growth. Stewardesses For Women's Rights was formed to meet a need created by the new consciousness among stewardesses."

SFWR now has regional chapters all across the country and is planning to hire a full time national staff. It has filed a series of antidiscrimination lawsuits against the airlines, and mounted a campaign to pressure the companies to take action on their "affirmative action" programs, which they are now required to develop to eliminate racial and sexual discrimination.

Stewardesses For Women's Rights is at the forefront of a widespread movement among flight attendants that has developed only over the past three years. Other groups, reacting to the same forces, are also demanding change.

One such group calls itself Mary Poppins, presumably because the fictional governess flew through the air with so much dignity. The group was formed in the summer of 1973 around a nucleus of twelve experienced stewardesses who opposed new policies by their airline that were aimed at forcing out older women. The airline had changed its "stand-by" regulation so that senior stewardesses were no longer exempt. After a series of stormy meetings attended by up to 200 stewardesses from that line, company officials rescinded the rule. The Mary Poppins people no longer feel intimidated.

The unions have been slow to respond to the new mood. The largest, the stewardess division of the Air Line Pilots Association, has scheduled seminars on the question of "The Image of the Stewardess" at its national convention over the past several years, but thus far the discussions have degenerated into confusion. As often as not, the panelists selected have ended up spouting the company line.

At the 1972 panel discussion on the "image" question, Mike Clark, a public relations man for National Airlines, unwittingly revealed some of the company's attitudes that are causing rebellion. "Your profession's worst enemy is the stewardess," he proclaimed. "I bet everyone in this room has flown with stewardesses too lazy or too indifferent to get the job done. But when the trip was over did you ever try to call these girls aside and say: 'Look, this isn't a bad job; straighten up,' or failing that, help your company get rid of these bad apples because you don't need them.

"But besides the bad apple," he continued, "there is a worse enemy and one much more difficult to control and one that is inside every one of you. . . . That enemy is the tendency to tell the world or any portion thereof, our troubles."

That is a wonderful expression of the company attitude —that all problems are caused by bad or neurotic stewardesses. It is an attitude that has been all too prevalent among the unions themselves.

But if the unions have been slow to understand what is happening, and have unwittingly allowed the most destructive kind of company propaganda to permeate their conferences, there has been a rebellion stirring here too.

Pilots outnumber stewardesses by 28,000 to 17,000 in ALPA, but some of the pilots, reacting to the new feminist mood, have developed an almost pathological fear that the women will take over. In 1972, pilots asked the ALPA stewardess division executive committee to consider changing the bylaws so that the stewardesses would have only an "affiliate" status. As far as the stewardesses could figure out, all this would mean was that they would lose the right to vote for the president of the union.

Rather than accept the change, the division consulted with the Labor Department and discovered that the manner in which the officers were currently being elected was illegal, and would have to be revised before the 1974 election.

But if some pilots want to get rid of the stewardesses, some stewardesses are hoping to separate from ALPA and create their own independent union.

Kelly Rueck, head of the Stewardess Division of ALPA, captured the mood of the new stewardess militancy in a speech before the executive board meeting in May of 1973.

"No longer is the stewardess position considered a 'way station,' a plateau along the line to another place," she declared. "It has developed into an occupation, a career that now has average tenure (for ALPA members) of five years, with one-third of our members married and many with children.

"With the shattering of discriminatory rules and requirements concerning age, marriage, and maternity, we begin to look forward to staying on the job and building our work into a career."

She went on to describe the new attitude of stewardesses, who no longer quietly acquiesce to company policies: "Now we question and probe the validity of rules that are forced on us with no apparent benefit to ourselves, the passengers, or the company."

Some perspectives on what it means to be a stewardess are being pieced together by people like Sandra Jarrell and David Roadhouse and Kelly Rueck. The central concept is that women are being exploited by the airline companies, that their sex is being used to merchandise airline tickets, that they are being treated in a dehumanizing way. But more and more women realize what is being done to them, and are preparing to rebel. Only instead of rebelling in small, personal ways, they are engaged in a general uprising that promises to quietly revolutionize the sex roles in the skies.

Sex Roles
in the Sky

In the hallway of the United Airlines Stewardess College near Chicago's O'Hare Field there is a bronze plaque dedicated to the first stewardess, Ellen Church. She is credited in the dedication with launching the "Sky Girls" in 1930 for Boeing Air Transport, predecessor company to United.

She was the first stewardess, and tradition has it that the graduating stewardesses used to rub the nose of the plaque for good luck when they started off on a flying career.

But nowhere on the plaque or in the public relations material put out by the airline does it mention that Ellen Church was a pilot, and that her ambition had been to fly planes for Boeing, not serve passengers in the cabin.

Ellen Church had wanted to be a pilot since as a young girl growing up in Cresco, Iowa, she had seen stunt pilot Ruth Law soar over the county fairgrounds in a primitive flying machine. She became a registered nurse, moved to

San Francisco, and took flying lessons. On February 23, 1930, she went to the Boeing Air Transport office to arrange a free flight back to Iowa for a visit, with the intention of getting a job with the airline if she could.

This was at a time when the airlines were mainly mail carriers, when there were fifteen stops between Chicago and San Francisco to deliver the mail, and when the struggling lines were trying desperately to interest a frightened public in air travel.

The San Francisco district manager of Boeing, Steve A. Stimpson, had just returned from Chicago on the airline's latest model, the Boeing 80. The trimotor plane was advertised as having "luxurious appointments," but Stimpson found the voyage very uncomfortable for the ten passengers on board. He ended up passing out lunches, serving the coffee, and trying to make the trip more comfortable for them. When he got to his office he wired his superiors urging them to add a steward, possibly a Filipino boy, to the crew.

That day Ellen Church came into his office to discuss her trip home. Most accounts of their meeting that afternoon describe how Ellen Church proposed that Boeing hire women instead of men as stewards, and how the two of them agreed to work together to create the first stewardess corps.

But that account didn't seem to ring entirely true. Ellen Church died in 1965, but Stimpson is living in Burbank, California, so I called him up to ask him exactly what transpired at that meeting. Had Ellen Church wanted to become a pilot?

"Yes, she did have some thoughts of becoming a co-pilot," Stimpson recalled. "But we agreed that day it would be better to try to sell Boeing on the idea of women as stewards."

The next day Stimpson sent off a letter proposing their joint idea.

"Imagine the psychology of having young women as regular members of the crew," the letter said. "Imagine the tremendous effect it would have on the traveling public. Also imagine the value that they would be to us in the neater and nicer method of serving food and looking out for the passengers.

"I am not suggesting at all the flapper type of girl. You know nurses as well as I do, and you know that they are not given to flightiness—I mean in the head. The average graduate nurse is a girl with some horse sense and is very practical. The young women that we select would naturally be intelligent and could handle what traffic work aboard was necessary, such as keeping records, filling out reports, issuing tickets, etc, etc."

The company heads eventually decided to give the idea a three-month trial on the Chicago to San Francisco run. The two of them were given just fifteen days to recruit seven more nurses as stewardesses, design the uniforms, and be ready to fly on an experimental basis.

Stimpson recalled that Eddie Rickenbacker, the World War I flying ace, had been very angry when he got wind of the idea. He flew out to San Francisco from Miami to try to talk Stimpson out of going ahead with his experiment.

"He asked me not to use the girls," Stimpson said. "He said, 'If you're going to put any help on at all, stay with men.'" Rickenbacker argued that flying was a man's occupation, and should stay that way.

But Stimpson held to his idea, the three-month experiment was launched, and despite initial resistance from the pilots, the idea spread. Within two years most of the other major airlines had followed suit and hired women as stewardesses.

Ellen Church stayed with the airline as head of the stewardesses for about a year, and then resigned. She returned to nursing, and during World War II she served as a captain in the Army Nurse Corps. She received the Army Air Medal for her services on flights carrying wounded men from Africa back to the United States. After the war she became administrator of the Union Hospital in Terre Haute, Indiana, and died there in 1965 after being thrown from a horse.

Ellen Church was proud of having helped open up a new career for women. United Airlines regularly called on her to appear at ceremonial occasions, and according to friends in Terre Haute, she was always happy to comply.

So these are the origins of the stewardess. It seems quite possible that if Ellen Church hadn't happened to come into the Boeing office that day, the airline might well have decided to use Filipino boys as stewards instead, or perhaps black porters, as the trains were then using.

But Stimpson and Church, with all the mixed motives apparent in Stimpson's letters, had created an institution that was to remain virtually unchanged for four decades. Men were pilots. Young women were stewardesses.

This institution spread worldwide, along with the new aircraft being poured out by American manufacturers. Most European airlines included men as well as women as flight attendants, but throughout the rest of the world the American model was usually followed precisely.

And from the beginning the roles were clearly arbitrary. In 1930 there was a remarkable number of women pilots. That was the year, for instance, when a young Englishwoman, Amy Johnson, set an endurance record by flying from London to Australia.

It wasn't until 1970 that male stewards starting joining stewardesses as flight attendants on all American airlines. It wasn't until 1973 that women copilots joined the men in the cockpit.

For all the questions raised by the establishment of these strict sexual roles, Stimpson and Church did open up a new career for women, a career that thousands of women took part in proudly over the next several decades.

During the 30's stewardesses were always registered nurses. They wore capes or long leather aviation coats, and uniforms with scarves around their necks. They looked adventuresome, and they must have been. Flying was still in its early stages, and emergencies cropped up with regularity. They did not look like models, and their grooming was typical of the professional woman, not the movie star.

It was a hard life, with low pay and working hours

that would not be tolerated today, and most stewardesses resigned after only a year or two. But it was a proud profession. Betty Friedan pointed out in *The Feminine Mystique* that in the 1930's and 40's our society looked up to the adventuresome woman. The magazine stories of 1939, she wrote, reflected an admiration for career women. "They were New Women," she said, "creating with a gay determined spirit a new identity for women— a life of their own."

They were "happily, proudly, adventurously, attractively career women—who loved and were loved by men."

Ellen Church was that kind of woman. And so was Jacqueline Cochran, who in 1939 wrote to Eleanor Roosevelt proposing that the Air Force enlist the services of women pilots for the war that then seemed inevitable. Mrs. Roosevelt persuaded her husband that it was a good idea, and from September 1942, to December 1944, Miss Cochran headed an auxiliary contingent of women pilots numbering up to 300, who transported planes from suppliers to military bases on the homefront.

But the unit was established over the strong objections of many military men, and finally gained approval only when there was a critical lack of pilots. Miss Cochran, meanwhile, had demonstrated the feasibility of the idea by flying with a similar women's unit in England, and Mrs. Roosevelt kept up a steady barrage of publicity on the subject in her regular newspaper column.

The unit was disbanded amidst controversy over its relations with the Air Force, and after there seemed to be enough men pilots to accomplish all the needed transportation. Of course none of the women pilots succeeded in finding employment with the commercial airlines.

Judging by a sampling of newspaper and magazine stories in the following years, it seems that stewardesses were considered glamorous, intelligent, and able. The requirement that they be nurses had been dropped by most of the airlines during the war out of necessity, but there was no indication of any lessening of respect for the job.

There was a fairly static period from the war years to the early 60's, when the stewardess uniform remained virtually unchanged, the turnover remained high, and the airlines maintained that the women left so soon because they were so eligible for marriage.

But a slow transformation was under way. More and more emphasis was placed on looks and glamour. Most of the airlines quietly adopted reassignment policies, requiring stewardesses to stop flying at age thirty-two or thirty-five. American Airlines adopted the cutoff age of thirty-two in 1953, and Braniff International in 1956.

Stewardesses were required to sign statements that they would voluntarily retire at the specified age. The purpose of these statements was more symbolic than real. Less than 3 percent of American Airline stewardesses were over thirty in the year 1967, and average tenure was just two years. But we knew from the beginning that the airline was offering us only a brief career. At least fourteen companies adopted similar forced retirement rules during the 1950's.

It was in the 1950's that a paramilitary regimen of hairdos and the precise shades of lipstick was introduced. On TWA, for instance, your lipstick had to match the red of the TWA emblem. The companies took the attitude that the high turnover was a sign of the quality of stewardesses. On some lines tenure was as low as eighteen months. "If it got up to thirty-five months," a United vice-president remarked in 1965, "I'd know we were getting the wrong kind of girl. She's not getting married."

But there was a shift to a much more explicit sexual image in 1966 when ad executive Mary Wells inspired Braniff's "end of the plain plane" campaign. Included in the campaign were jet planes decked out in seven different shades of pastel colors, and exotic new stewardess wardrobes by the Italian designer Pucci. This was soon followed by the "Braniff Air Strip," with stewardesses required to go through a series of flashy costume changes, ending up in hot pants.

Other airlines soon followed suit. Western introduced flowing high fashion lounging pajamas. California's Pacific Southwest Airline dressed stewardesses in celery-green miniskirts with hot orange peekaboo pettipants. Alaska Airlines featured Gay Nineties flights, with stewardesses in ankle-length red velvet dresses and 1890's hair styles. These stewardesses had to sing in-flight announcements to Calamity Jane lyrics. Lake Central stewardesses wore "Love at first flight" buttons.

The image was shifting from that of an attractive wife-to-be (with all the inherent limitations that that implied) to a much more sexually explicit Playboy

Bunny or torch singer. A new wave of books began cashing in on the new imagery, starting with *Coffee, Tea, or Me?* which was ghost-written in 1967 by a former public relations man for American Airlines.

This new image had direct results on the planes. Pinching and patting increased. "They might get a pat, but the girls are moving so fast they scarcely have time to get pinched," an American supervisor volunteered cheerily in early 1967. Dell Mott, now air safety coordinator for the stewardess division of ALPA, recalls that a wave of pinching started that year in response to the new image.

Enforcing passenger discipline became more and more of a problem. On a charter flight of Southern Airlines that year, men returning to Atlanta from a professional football game pursued the stewardesses so actively that the women had to take refuge in the cockpit, and the pilot made a forced landing.

The image of the sexual stewardess was flowering at the same time that a series of court rulings and EEOC decisions were laying the groundwork for a transformation of the job. The major gains for the rights of flight attendants, involving marriage, age, maternity leave, and hiring of black stewardesses and male stewards, were won in a seemingly endless series of hearings and lawsuits, complaints and appeals based on the anti-discrimination provision of the 1964 Civil Rights Act.

Similar cases resulted in the airlines being forced to drop marriage or children as valid grounds for dismissal, and the EEOC issued an advisory decision in 1968 that sex was not a bona fide occupational qualification. After a similar period of delays and appeals, stewards started joining the airlines in force in 1972.

There were economic factors involved in the airlines' increasing exploitation of women. The airlines are the most heavily regulated transportation industry. Prices and routes are controlled by the Civil Aeronautics Board. The Board awarded an unprecedented number of new routes to the airlines in the late 1950's and the early 1960's with the hope of spurring competition. The airlines, with identical routes and identical fares, focused more and more attention on their stewardesses. They were the only distinguishing mark of the company, the employees with most contact with the customer.

But there is irony in the fact that the most exploitative advertising and publicity have come at the same time as the industry is being forced into a radical transformation, women are increasingly reexamining their traditional roles, and the women's liberation movement is being revived from the feminism of the 1920's.

Stimpson is not fond of the new sexy image of stewardesses. "Cheap," he said bitterly.

♀ Female Pilot, Male Steward

LAST year the *New Yorker* magazine carried a cartoon showing a group of anxious and startled businessmen staring into space as the announcement was being made on the intercom: "Welcome aboard. This is your captain, Margaret Williamson, speaking."

That same month, on February 6, 1973, a thirty-three-year-old pilot named Emily Howell was the third officer on a Frontier Airlines Boeing 737 flight from Denver to St. Louis, becoming the first woman pilot on a scheduled American airline.

We often make jokes about subjects that make us nervous, and it seems fair to say that the American psyche received a jolt in its sexual stereotypes in 1973. Three women became pilots—one at Frontier, one at American Airlines, and one at Eastern Airlines. And male stewards joined the airlines, making up as much as 20 percent of the graduating classes at the flight attendant schools.

The roles that had become so firmly established—of

male pilot and young woman stewardess—had been shattered, a full forty-three years after Ellen Church helped establish stewardess as a woman's occupation.

It is ironic that Ellen Church first hoped to become a pilot, and ended up becoming the first stewardess while Emily Howell, the first commercial airline pilot, originally dreamed of becoming a stewardess!

Emily Howell is now a copilot for Frontier, helping to fly a tiny Twin-Otter that seats just nineteen passengers. The plane has no partition between cabin and cockpit, and the passengers can clearly see that a woman is seated beside a man at the instrument panel. Ms. Howell says she is getting a lot of comments from passengers.

After one of her first flights into Denver a woman said: "I'm all for women's lib, but I must admit I was a little nervous." Ms. Howell replied: "Me too, lady."

It will be from five to ten years before she can become a captain but a spokesman at Frontier was absolutely certain she would make it. "She is going to be the first woman airline captain in the country," he said with pride. "She's got a head start on the women at American and Eastern."

In fact, the airlines have become very competitive about their women pilots. A spokesman for American Airlines asserted that Emily Howell wasn't really a pilot at all, and that American's Bonnie Linda Tiburzi was truly the first pilot. The company even took out a full page ad in *Ms.* magazine, reproducing the *New Yorker* cartoon and declaring, "We were the first major airline with a woman pilot." Meanwhile, over at Eastern Airlines, a spokesman pointed out that Barbara Banett, who flew her first scheduled flight for that company in August of 1973, was in a way the first woman pilot because she had flown charter planes for the Zantop company out of Detroit two years ago.

But the fact remains that Emily Howell was the first woman pilot for a regularly scheduled domestic airline.

Ms. Howell says she became a pilot for the most practical of reasons: the airlines provide a good salary and job security. She came from a family of six that had some hard times financially. Her father was a truck driver in Denver, and she and her twin sister were born at a time when there just weren't enough beds in the house, and one of them slept in a cardboard box.

She started working part-time at fourteen, and full time as soon as she graduated from Holy Family High School in Denver. She worked as a saleswoman in a Denver department store until 1957, when she became fascinated with flying on a short flight from Gunnison to Denver. The crew invited her to join them in the cockpit, and the copilot suggested that if she enjoyed it so much she should take flying lessons. That year she went to work for the Clinton Aviation Company as a flight school secretary. By 1959 she managed to get her private pilot's license, and by 1961 her commercial and flight instructor's rating.

She stayed with the Clinton Company for fifteen years, becoming the flight school manager and chief pilot, and a Federal Aviation Administration examiner. By the time she joined Frontier she had logged 7,100 flying hours.

"But even when I was in flight training I still wanted to be a stewardess," she said. She also modeled for a Denver modeling school, and entered the Queen of Colorado beauty pageant in 1960.

She doesn't feel that there is any contradiction between her desire to be a stewardess and her modeling and the fact that she ended up as the first woman to become a commercial airline pilot. She simply points out: "I didn't win the beauty contest." She is divorced and lives with her eight-year-old son. Her twin sister is a nurse and a captain in the U.S. Air Force.

"The equal opportunity laws have changed the atmosphere in the country," she said. They helped pave the way for her eventual acceptance as a pilot. The job did not come easily. She first applied in 1967, and returned in September 1972, when she heard a rumor that Frontier was hiring.

"I went back every couple of weeks to see how my application was doing," she recalls. "Finally, in January they called me in for an interview. I told them, 'I'm not going to sue you for a job. I just really want to be a pilot.' " She got the job.

At first some of the pilots gave her a difficult time. One pilot ignored the fact that she was there during an entire flight. "I rode it out all right," Emily said. Most of the pilots seemed very cautious at first, waiting to see how things would work out. But the ice was broken after a few months, and they have become very helpful. "Now that I'm in, they'd like to see me make it," she continued. Even the pilot who ignored her on that flight has become

much more friendly. "I'm very pleased with the men—
the reception they have given me. They'll go overboard,
even though they feel threatened."

The stewardesses also tended to be cool at first, and
many of them seemed to think it was a publicity stunt,
but she feels they have come to accept her also.

Ms. Howell did not consider herself a member of the
women's liberation movement when I first interviewed
her in August of 1973. "I think a lot of it is too much,"
she stated. "Strong women make inroads. You work
hard and show what you're worth, without raising Cain."

But early in 1974 she had changed her mind. "For the
first time, women are making it all over," she said. "The
women's movement is really changing things." It was the
women's movement that paved the way for dramatic
changes in the airlines. It was a series of antidiscrimination rulings on hard fought cases that created the climate
for women to finally be hired as pilots.

And it was an antidiscrimination suit filed by a Miami
man in 1967 that finally ended with a Supreme Court
ruling in 1971 that men could not be denied jobs as
flight attendants on the basis of their sex.

Now every major airline is hiring male stewards, and
the percentage of men in the flight training schools av-
erages between 15 and 20 percent, depending on the airline.

Most of the men seem to have the same kind of practical economic considerations for becoming stewards as
Emily Howell had for becoming a pilot. Many have
come from other jobs in the airline industry, such as

ticket agent or ramp loader. Most of them intend to make a career with the airline, and see their job as a temporary interlude that may improve their chances for upward mobility into management.

Ramiro de la Garza has been flying six months for American Airlines, and he says he loves the job. He is a good example of the practical steward. He had already worked for five years with the company as a ramp loader and ticket agent before becoming a steward and plans to remain with American for his working career. "I think everyone should move around a bit," he said. He comes from an airline family. His father worked for American in Monterey, Mexico, and then in Chicago, and his brother is a flight service director for the company.

An official at United Airlines had told me how men were selected on precisely the same basis as women. They were looking for men who wanted to spend a few years flying before settling down. But it still amazed me talking to Ramiro to realize that the companies were treating the stewards so much like sex objects, and that the stewards seemed to be prepared to adapt to that role.

In flight training school, Ramiro said, the men were excused from some of the grooming classes. But they still brought in a hair stylist to cut their hair, and still suggested a whole line of cosmetics for male use, ranging from colognes to deodorants and facial washes. They still modified the way the men walked, in Ramiro's case, having him hold his head higher.

But there's no question that Ramiro is enjoying his new role. "This job can really go to your head," he said.

"You get so many compliments you don't know how to react. One day a woman passenger just went on and on. 'Boy did you miss yours,' she said. 'You ought to be on television or in the movies.' "

"One lady asked me what hotel I was staying at in Indianapolis," he continued. "It was the first time I had been there, and I really didn't know. She said, 'Well, I'll be at the Holiday Inn.' "

He enjoys dating stewardesses and passengers both. "I really enjoy working with the girls," Ramiro commented. "It's the best part of the job."

Other stewards seem to have similar reactions. United Airlines's Cliff Cooley relates how he was asked out by a member of a Roller Derby team, and took her up on it. He also says he has been the victim of a classic role reversal—he has been pinched on his way down the aisle.

These stewards are still in the "honeymoon" stage of flying, and their romanticism can be expected to fade. Ramiro conceded that he might be reevaluating the job in the future. "Right now I'm enjoying it a lot; maybe in a year from now I'll find it hard."

There are already some signs that the new stewards will affect the job in the years ahead. For one thing, the men, who have presumably been raised to be more assertive, often refuse to put up with as much harassment from the passengers and the crew.

Some pilots have been very cool to the new stewards. One of Ramiro's friends was given a hard time by a pilot who made a few jokes about his possible lack of masculinity. When his friend took his jacket off while serving the meal the pilot insisted that he put it back on. When he refused, the pilot ordered him to put his jacket on, thundering, "I'm in command here."

A short while later the captain asked for a Coke, and the steward refused to serve him. "There is no place in my contract that says I have to serve you," he said.

Another friend actually poured a cocktail over the head of a male passenger who was giving him a difficult time, Ramiro says. One passenger started imitating Ramiro in a high pitched feminine voice. He went over to the man and said calmly, "Wait a minute, pal. Let's get something straight. Either you cut that out or we'll have words when we get off this airplane."

Many of the stewards believe that being a cabin attendant is a full time profession, a profession that the airlines should demonstrate more respect for. One steward for United, John Siepen, is in the unique position of having been a second officer for the airline. He was laid off in April of '71, and was one of the two or three pilots who accepted United's offer to become stewards until they were recalled.

"The job is more demanding, mentally and physically, than a pilot's," he said. "I really have a lot more respect for the job than I did before.

"I know that stewardesses have gotten the reputation of being unfriendly, snippy, but it's the airlines' own fault. To keep up with the competition they just keep building up the work load."

He thinks that the airlines are unrealistic in expecting stewards and stewardesses to smile no matter what a passenger does. "They could reach out and sock you in the nose and you're supposed to smile and say, 'Oh thank you, sir, thanks,' " he said. "Sometimes you just want to explode. I go into the buffet area and throw things."

Nineteen hundred and seventy-three was the year that women flew airplanes, and male flight attendants had temper tantrums in the galley.

 *Safety*

THE Convair jet was coming in for a landing across Long Island Sound to New Haven Airport in a thick fog. The flight recorder transcribed the following conversation:

Captain: "Keep a real sharp eye out there."

First officer: "Okay."

Captain: "Oh, this is low."

First officer: "You can't see down through this stuff."

Captain: "I can see the water."

First officer: "Ah, yeah, I can see the water. We're right over the water."

First officer: "Man, we ain't twenty feet off the water."

Captain: "Hold it."

One second later there is the sound of impact.

On June 7, 1971, Allegeny Airlines Flight 485 crashed into three beach cottages at 9:49 A.M. while attempting an instrument landing at the New Haven Airport, coming to rest a little short of a mile from the runway. There were twenty-six adult passengers, two infants, two pilots, and one stewardess aboard the flight. Twenty-eight persons died.

The National Transportation Safety Board determined from its investigation that this was a "survivable" crash. The cockpit was demolished, but the passengers and stewardess were alive when the plane bellied into the marshes beyond the waterfront beach cottages. Why did they die?

There were three major reasons given in the NTSB report. The airline had been granted an exemption by the Federal Aviation Administration to have only one instead of two stewardesses aboard. The one stewardess was badly injured on initial impact. The passengers could not open the complicated rear door themselves, and because of the darkness and dense smoke in the cabin, could not read the instructions.

Several witnesses testified that they heard voices of people in the craft near the rear exit, before a series of violent explosions racked the fuselage. The bodies of fourteen passengers and the stewardess were found near the rear service door.

This particular accident is a good illustration of some of the major causes of airline crash fatalities in recent years. Some 90 percent of modern-day crashes are judged "survivable" by the NTSB, and yet all too often the passengers and crew do not survive.

The reasons that contributed to the fatalities in the New Haven crash were similar to the reasons for deaths on a series of airplane crashes before and since that accident: an inadequate number of trained stewardesses; dangerous jump seats and seating locations for stewardesses; cabin materials that do not burn, but produce a thick, poisonous smoke.

"With the exception of the captain, who sustained fatal injuries upon impact," the board's report read, "everyone aboard this flight could have survived if rapid egress from the fire area had been possible or if flame propagation had been retarded.

"The problem of rapid egress is most prominent," the report continued. "The stewardess is called upon and relied upon for assistance to the passengers in an emergency. In this case, as in so many other cases, such assistance may not have been possible due to a partially incapacitating injury which was inflicted upon the cabin attendant at impact."

Yes, as in "so many other cases," the stewardess was seriously injured on impact, due to a continuing indifference on the part of the airline companies to the safety of flight attendants.

The stewardess, twenty-seven-year-old Judith L. Manning, suffered more than a "partially incapacitating injury" on impact. According to the NTSB report she suffered "fractures of the upper posterior rib, fracture of the left clavicle, and fracture of the third thoracic vertebra." She died of carbon monoxide and cyanide poisoning from the fumes of the burning cabin.

The NTSB report made several safety recommendations as a result of its analysis of the crash, the most important of which were: to provide adequate shoulder harnesses for stewardesses, improved warning systems for stewardesses, and a strong recommendation that the FAA not grant any more exemptions for the number of stewardesses required to be on board.

"Although cabin attendants' seating arrangements and restraining devices presently used might not have prevented injury to a second stewardess," the report said, "the board believes that the possibility for a greater number of survivors would have existed had a second cabin attendant been aboard this flight."

The NTSB has recognized the dangerous flying conditions for stewardesses, and the danger that this presents to the safety of all passengers. Every experienced stewardess also knows the dangers of sitting on collapsible jump seats, in galleys with loose equipment—wherever the companies position them in the nooks and crannies of the craft. But nothing is done about it. The "survivable accidents" continue to claim victims.

Seven months earlier, on November 27, 1970, a Capitol International Airways DC-8 crashed following an unsuccessful takeoff attempt from Anchorage, Alaska. The flight was a troop transport on the way to South Vietnam, with 219 military passengers and a crew of ten on board.

Forty-six passengers and one stewardess died in the fire that followed the crash.

Again the NTSB found that the crash was "survivable," that most of the deaths were due to carbon monoxide and cyanide poisoning from the burning cabin interior, and that escape from the cabin was hindered by the fact that all five surviving stewardesses on board were injured during the initial impact.

"Cabin interior design features were directly involved in injuries and incapacitation of flight crew attendants and in some instances these features restricted the evacuation routes within the cabin," the NTSB report read.

The Board is extremely concerned that the cabin attendants, who are depended upon and are responsible for emergency assistance to passengers, were either partially or totally incapacitated during this accident.

"Of particular concern," the NTSB report concluded, "are improvements in the crashworthiness of galley equipment, stewardess seats, and restraining devices, and the flammability of cabin interior materials."

But the NTSB does not have any power. It can only make recommendations to the Federal Aviation Administration. And the FAA failed to act.

On March 3, 1972, a Mohawk Airlines Fairchild, with forty-five passengers and a crew of three, crashed into a house three and a half miles short of the Albany County Airport. Fourteen passengers and the two pilots died in the crash. The stewardess was injured, as were thirty-one passengers.

The safety board found the accident "partially survivable," and said the single stewardess on board "received injuries caused by the collapse of her seat and by striking her head on the door ... actuating mechanism." Among the board's findings was that "the design and location of the stewardess' seat did not afford crashworthiness protection."

The list could go on. The point is that if you are a passenger in a "survivable" accident, the chances are good that you will not survive because your stewardesses are injured and cannot perform their most important task—directing the emergency evacuation of the plane. If you are a stewardess in a "survivable" accident, the chances are very good that you will be either severely injured or killed.

The dangers of the jump seats and the galley equipment are no secret. Virtually every experienced stewardess is concerned with the way the flight attendant seats are hidden away in the dangerous, unusable corners of aircraft.

On the Boeing 727-100, one stewardess seat has been shifted from a passenger seat, 9C, to a jump seat partially inside the coat compartment, and finally to a jump seat in the galley, the most dangerous place conceivable, surrounded by hundreds of pounds of kitchen equipment.

On one month's flights in 1969, when the seat was located by the coat compartment, I would sit in seat 9C instead. Even when an FAA inspector came on board, I refused to sit in my assigned place, although I knew it could be grounds for dismissal.

I went up to him and asked, "What do you think of my not sitting in that jump seat? I don't have my padded suit and crash helmet on." He said, "I don't blame you." After that month, I never bid that position on a 727-100 again.

In November of 1970 the ALPA Stewards and Stewardesses Division released a study it had conducted of what happens in the cabin of an aircraft during an accident. The report concluded:

"It was shocking to note that of the total number of

eighty-one reports examined for 1968, 1969, and 1970, thirty-nine were found to be pertinent to the research and from these thirty-nine, there were nineteen instances of injuries to flight attendants during turbulence, twenty-three instances of galley equipment dislodging, blocking, or otherwise hampering emergency evacuation, and eighteen instances of baggage or other debris blocking the aisles and/or exits. These facts in themselves are sufficient evidence that the cabin attendant's working conditions are extremely hazardous and that immediate action must be taken toward improvement."

The study also found that many stewardesses escaped injury by refusing to sit in their jump seats, and that "in many instances if the attendant had occupied her assigned jump seat, the debris, equipment, etc., in her seating area not only would have hampered her leadership of the evacuation, but also might have severely injured her."

How can the airlines allow these conditions to continue year after year? Veteran members of the NTSB investigation team still recall the days when the airline companies would rush their employees to the scene of an accident to paint over the company name on the plane for fear they would lose business as a result of the publicity. The practice finally ended in the early 1950's when the press made a point of revealing the names of the companies and describing their efforts to cover up their identity.

But the days of paint buckets were indicative of an attitude that still prevails on the airlines. Plane crashes do not happen. Safety precautions cost money. Interiors must be designed to attract customers, not to be crash-worthy. Stewards and stewardesses must be placed where no paying customer would want to sit.

But planes do crash, and passengers and crew do die.

According to figures compiled by the National Safety Council your chances of being killed on a trip from New York to Chicago are slightly higher on a plane than on an interstate bus, and only slightly lower than on a passenger train.

From 1970 through 1972, the fatality rate per 100 million passenger miles was .09 for intercity buses, .28 for passenger trains, and .10 for regularly scheduled domestic flights. A reseacher at the safety council said the railroad figure was actually inflated, since several commuter train wrecks occured in 1972 that should not be included in this comparison.

Until recently the trend had been that airplane travel was becoming safer. During the 1950's and early '60's, plane travel had been considerably more dangerous than either train or bus, but steadily improved until 1971, when planes were the safest means of transportation.

But since 1971 the passenger plane fatality rate has begun climbing again. According to the National Transportation Safety Board, the accident rate per 100,000 flight hours, for national and international flights, climbed from .094 in 1971, to .127 in 1972, and .138 in 1973.

According to the board's figures, 227 persons died in nine accidents involving scheduled air carriers last year, compared with 190 people in eight accidents the year before.

Capt. Vernon W. Lowell pointed out in his book, *Airline Safety is a Myth,* published in 1967, that there are several quirks in the statistics that make comparisons difficult. But even taken at face value, he pointed out, the airline safety statistics are misleading because a plane goes so much faster than buses or trains. On an hour-for-hour basis, he calculated, it was twenty times safer to be in a bus, and thirty times safer in a train.

Another example of negligence on the part of the airlines is the type of material currently being used for cabin interiors. Many of these new fabrics were designed to be noninflammable, but give off a dense black smoke containing deadly cyanide fumes.

In 1969, the FAA issued an advance notice of proposed rulemaking in order to "establish standards governing the smoke-emission characteristics of aircraft interior materials." The notice stated that "aircraft crashworthiness would be significantly upgraded if smoke emission from burning interior materials could be reduced in sufficient measure."

But to date no such rule has been issued. And the office of Aviation Medicine of the FAA on January 29, 1973, released a report that cited four accidents in which cyanide was often present in the bloodstreams of victims in amounts that would be incapacitating and frequently fatal. The four accidents cited were the Anchorage, Alaska, crash; the New Haven, Connecticut, crash; and two crashes in Chicago in 1972.

Ralph Nader's Aviation Consumer Action Project has filed an appearance in the FAA docket on the proposed rule change as a result of the Midway air crash on December 8, 1972, in Chicago. Seven persons died in that crash as a result of cyanide poisoning, the petition says.

"People in aircraft accidents have died, in great and increasing numbers," the petition reads, "from the inhalation of smoke and toxic gases emitted from burning cabin interiors; people who would have lived in the absence of such smoke and gases."

Industry representatives have filed materials with FAA, denying that there is any danger in the cabin materials currently in use.

"If the fuel of the aircraft is ignited at the time of impact and the fire involves the cabin interior, the likelihood that your regulations ... will result in a safer environment is so remote as to make your whole proposal a fantastically expensive and futile exercise," said the comment from one manufacturing firm.

"The extent of the need for smoke emission performance standards to promote increased safety in aircraft has not, as yet, been determined," commented the Society of the Plastics Industry, Inc.

But the fact is that passengers and crew have died from the thick, deadly smoke of burning cabin interiors, and that safer materials, including plastics which produce "only a tiny fraction" of the cyanide under similar fire conditions, are already available, according to the FAA's own office of Aviation Medicine. And yet the FAA has failed to act.

The only explanation is that the FAA is controlled by people who care more about big business than the public, more about profit margins than safety. Congressman Jack Brooks of Texas, who for years has been trying to improve safety in the transportation of hazardous materials, concluded that the FAA is just plain incompetent. "The FAA is probably one of the most interesting, fascinating, and worst agencies in the government," he said on a CBS interview, "run by nice, pleasant people. They have nice airplanes; they are courteous; they're really very personable folks; utterly incompetent."

There are a lot of other situations permitted by FAA that aggravate stewardesses. For instance on the DC-10's, ten stewardesses are maximum on board, but only five have to be trained on that model of plane. The other five would only tend to get in the way in an emergency. Similarly, on the 747's the requirement is that only seven of the fourteen stewardesses on the craft have to be trained for that plane.

On the 727-200, one stewardess is seated in a passenger's seat at the back end of the plane, but, in case of an emergency, she is expected to walk along the arm rests of the seats to a forward window exit. It's a certainty that the stewardess is not going to be able to make it up the aisle by hopping from arm rest to arm rest.

There are other, minor safety hazards confronted regularly by stewardesses. There are coffee machines that sometimes explode. A friend of mine spent hours picking the coffee grounds out of her skin after one such explosion. There are oxygen tanks that sometimes explode. At one point we were all directed to take the oxygen tanks into the galley before opening them because there was a danger of explosion. Small comfort to the person who has to open them.

The most frustrating aspect of all these safety problems

is the total disregard by our employers. I must have sent twenty letters to superiors during my years of flying, detailing problems with jump seats, galley equipment, and cabin materials. But we simply are not listened to. I never received a response.

The airlines and the federal regulatory agencies have exhibited an utter disregard for the safety of flight attendants, and therefore, indirectly, for the safety of passengers.

Only the NTSB, an independent agency whose sole function is to investigate accidents and make recommendations to the FAA, has consistently recognized the dangers to stewardesses caused by inadequate FAA regulations. And the NTSB reports seem to have a ring of desperation, as if they realize the effort is futile.

Why hasn't the FAA done anything? According to Neil McBride, the attorney who runs Ralph Nader's Consumer Action Program, the problem lies with confusion in the role that FAA thinks it should play. The FAA administrators see their mission as both promoting the airline industry and assuring safety to the public. The two roles are not as compatible as they might first appear, one said, and in fact the FAA has become a servant of the industry.

Health

THERE are many improvements that could be made on airplanes that would make the job of stewardess a lot easier and a lot healthier. Most of these improvements involve very little money or effort. They have not been made because of the airlines' indifference to health questions, and because until recently stewardesses were generally too submissive to demand improvements.

In recent months Stewardesses For Women's Rights has become increasingly concerned with these health questions, and has started the laborious task of tracking down what information is already available on such questions as oxygen supply in pressurized cabins, humidity levels in the new jumbo jets, and the effects of jet lag and disorganized working conditions on the mind.

In May of 1968 the Air France medical department published a study of the psychological and physical effects of being an airline stewardess, based on 300 psychiatric examinations involving 151 Air France stewardesses.

The paper described widespread states of "anxiety and frustration" which it concluded were related to what has come to be known as "jet lag," and to the nature of the job on board the plane.

The study revealed that there was a general state of mental fatigue among the stewardesses, and that this state was probably related to a whole series of causes: "excessive task-loading with trivia, frequent emergencies or false alarms, inadequate compensation for task, inadequate recognition of accomplishments, inadequate task challenge and interest, ambiguous rules and procedures..."

The report is not particularly helpful in pinning down specific causes of stress, but it is somehow reassuring to know that those 151 Air France stewardesses experienced the same frustration with the job that we American stewardesses are all familiar with.

That report was contained in the files of Dwight Dedmon, until recently the health and safety expert for the Air Line Stewards and Stewardesses Association in Chicago. One of his reports deals with some purely physical aspects of flying.

According to Dedmon, the average oxygen deficiency in the cabin of a jet aircraft ranges from 14 to 16 percent below normal levels. When combined with a normal work load, it causes strain on the heart, swelling of the legs, and exhaustion. Continuous work under these conditions leads to "a deterioration of general health, particularly anemia," his report said.

Dedmon says that studies for the new French supersonic transport plane, the Concorde, were conducted on the premise that relative humidity should be at least 30 percent. And yet, he says, a survey of the levels of relative humidity in the cabins of American jet passenger planes indicates that the relative humidity is often as low as from 5 to 8 percent. This results in eye irritation, dehydration of the mucous membranes, and eventually a depletion of the body's supply of potassium, he says.

Another health problem is jet lag, or the difficulty that the body has in adapting to time zone changes. This is a complicated concept related to the body's adaptation to the earth's rotation on its axis. If you take a flight skipping over several time zones, your body will have a very difficult time adjusting to the new time and location. And, strangely, the difficulty involved is directly related to whether you are traveling in the same direction as the earth's rotation, or in the opposite direction.

A study by the Federal Aviation Administration's Office of Aviation Medicine describes the effects of one trip this way:

"a. Adverse physiological and biochemical changes produced by the outbound trip took up to five days to come into phase with local time.

"b. Those required by the inbound trip required only up to thirty-six hours.

"c. Intellectual and personality impairment resulting from the outbound trip was of much shorter duration than the physical impairment, requiring up to thirty-six hours for adjustment. Similarly, the inbound psychological adjustment period was also less.

"d. The combined effect of time-zone displacement and prolonged flight produced significantly more impairment than prolonged flight alone."

T.S. Banes, in a report to the Air Navigation Commission in March of 1966, concluded that the physical and psychological effects of jet lag can have serious effects on job performance.

"At the root of the subjective reaction described is an exhaustion, a weariness, perhaps a low-grade dissociation from reality, which cannot be altogether overcome by an effort of will. Characteristically, it is said, the subject will be prepared to accept lower-than-normal standards of performance; however, unless he has prior knowledge of the nature of time-shift effects, he is unlikely to recognize his mental impairment as such."

Dedmon argues that these and other difficulties of flying lead directly to a physical and mental fatigue characterized by irregular and insufficient sleep, digestive problems, and anemia. These physical problems in turn lead to "loss of professional motivation, personality deterioration, stress, and neurotic disorders."

He recommends a series of practical steps that could be taken to alleviate these problems, including an adjustment in work schedules and work loads, the maintenance of at least 30 percent humidity on board planes, and the maintenance of higher levels of oxygen.

I am not a medical expert, and I'm certainly not an expert on such questions as jet lag or oxygen and potassium levels. But it seems that Dedmon and the experts from France and Germany that he cites in his study, are taking a rational approach to some of the problem working conditions on the job.

And certainly the conditions described in these reports are familiar to every stewardess. I remember countless times when my eyes and nose and throat would get all dried up during a flight. We all seemed extra sensitive to colds and respiratory infections. When I had my tonsils taken out my doctor said that tonsilitis is a typical stewardess problem caused by dehydration on the airplane.

The lack of oxygen is also a familiar problem. I can't remember how many times I strapped myself into my jump seat as we came in for a landing totally exhausted. I remember walking through the plane on an all night flight like a zombie—not asleep, not awake—and then siting down on my jump seat. The next thing I remembered was my face hitting the floor as I toppled over.

I asked Dedmon how difficult it would be for the airlines to adjust the humidity and oxygen levels in the cabin. He said it wasn't a question of how difficult, because the companies were fully aware of these problems. Some experimental planes have had extra humidifiers to keep the moisture levels comfortable, he said, but they have always been dropped in the final models for reasons of cost. Similarly, he said, the level of oxygen could easily be raised with oxygen tanks. It isn't that these items would be so expensive, Dedmon said, but simply that the airlines can get away with cutting the corners because there is no organized resistance.

The people who suffer most directly are the stewards

and stewardesses—the only people who have to actively work during the flights, and the people who have the least power to demand changes.

Some measures could be taken to alleviate these conditions that wouldn't cost the airlines anything. For instance, we could at least be warned of what to look out for and what medications might help. But the airlines have instead taken their traditional position that the problems simply don't exist.

It seems clear that changes will be made only when stewardess organizations can mount enough strength to demand them.

☿ Radiation
on Passenger Planes

AN estimated one out of every ten flights originating in the United States carries radioactive materials in the cargo bin below the passenger cabin. In cities which are centers for the processing of radioactive isotopes for medical purposes, over half the flights may carry radioactive materials.

The legal limits for the amount of radiation dosage to passengers and crew permit more exposure than the general public is allowed to receive in any other public place. And these legal limits are routinely exceeded, as a study conducted for the Atomic Energy Commission confirmed in the summer of 1973.

Passengers and stewardesses have been exposed to doses of radiation on a single flight that far exceed what nuclear experts have established as the maximum safe exposure for a full year. There is reason to believe that these doses of radioactive isotopes have had a particular

133

effect on stewardesses, who spend some 900 hours a year in the plane cabins.

In fact, the Airline Pilots Association has gathered evidence that indicates that stewardesses stationed in certain cities may have a much higher rate of miscarriages and deformed children as a result of this radiation exposure. There is also some evidence that flight crews, freight handlers, and regular airline passengers in these cities can be expected to suffer a slightly higher incidence of leukemia and cancer.

This is obviously a very sensitive and frightening area that requires the most careful scientific study. And yet, because of the complexities of the issue and the lack of scientific certainty concerning the effects of low dosages of radiation, the federal regulatory agencies and the airlines themselves have refused to acknowledge the fact that these shipments are dangerous.

In February of 1972, after congressional testimony concerning illegal shipments of radioactive materials and the potential medical hazards involved, the Federal Aviation Administration issued a new interpretation of the regulations which actually increased the dosage a person could legally receive on a plane by more than three times, from 5.1 millirem an hour to 18.

Only a series of lawsuits by a Ralph Nader consumer group and continued pressure from ALPA caused FAA to modify its new rule, and finally, on October 1, 1973, after pressure from the U.S. Department of Health, Education, and Welfare, the FAA withdrew the rule altogether and returned to the antiquated rule in effect in 1971.

"FAA took action," their press release said, "after receiving a letter in August from the Department of Health, Education, and Welfare . . . suggesting that additional data was needed to further evaluate the public health aspects of the rule."

The FAA and the Atomic Energy Commission now say they are looking into the matter further, but their attitude is not reassuring. A spokesman for the FAA said that the agency relies on the AEC on such technical matters. A spokesman for the AEC said an attempt will be made to determine how many flights carry radioactive materials, and if the number of shipments warrants it, then a more restrictive rule will be developed. In other words, if it can be statistically shown that a meaningful number of people are being harmed by radioactivity on airplanes, then the rule will be changed. And there is reason to doubt the medical assumptions being used by the AEC to compute these probabilities.

Surely the only rational thing to do at this juncture is to either bar the transportation of these materials on passenger planes altogether, as they are now barred from buses, or to develop regulations that would limit radiation emissions to a negligible level. The only disadvantage of such regulations would be the cost of packaging. And yet the AEC continues to try to weigh the "cost-benefit" equation involved. How much does human life weigh in such an equation?

The airlines have apparently been aware of the potential hazards for some time. In 1962 the major airlines proposed to the Civil Aeronautics Board that they be exempt from any damages that might be caused by "nuclear reaction or nuclear radiation or radioactive contamination."

CAB rejected the request, noting, "We perceived no public policy considerations which require air carriers to be free from responsibility for damage caused or contributed to by their negligence, or indeed, their willful acts."

But if the airlines were aware of a potential problem, the general public and even the flight crews were not. The issue only came to public attention as a result of the efforts of two pilots for a small midwestern airline who stumbled on the question of the transportation of hazardous materials in May of 1971.

The two, Capt. James Eckels and Capt. Donald Dunn, were flying Fairchild prop jets, small crafts that seat some forty-five passengers. Each evening the seats would be removed and the body of the plane filled with cargo that was stacked in full view of the flight crews.

"We began to notice these boxes of hazardous materials," Captain Dunn recalled. "Some pilots would refuse to take off until the boxes were removed."

The airline's station agent assured the pilots that the shipments were routine and perfectly safe. But Eckels and Dunn were not satisfied. They poured over the regulations and discovered that some 90 percent of the shipments were illegal. They became particularly concerned with the illegal shipments of radioactive materials, which were supposed to be carefully limited according to the number of transport indexes contained in each package.

A transport index is the dose of radioactive isotopes received at a distance of three feet from the surface of a package. Any single package was limited to ten transport indexes, or TI, and planes could carry from one to fifty TI, depending on the size of the craft and the distance from the passengers and crew above the cargo bins.

Eckels and Dunn found loads on their planes far in excess of these limits. Only twenty TI were allowed on a DC-9 passenger plane, they determined, and yet they tabulated loads of 94.1, 35.7, 68.3, and 114.9 TI on separate flights.

They brought their findings to company officials. "They just told us we didn't know what we were talking about," Dunn related. "They told us to go soak our heads."

The two captains did not go and soak their heads. Instead, they devoted all their energies over the next six months to trying to determine just how much of a health hazard was involved in these shipments. They took photographs of packages containing the radioactive materials on the freight docks of seven different airlines. They would walk onto the freight dock at 3 or 4 A.M., say they were from ALPA, look around for illegal shipments, and snap the pictures before they were hustled out of the area by supervisors. They checked the docks of six airlines, and flew up to Chicago and visited the docks of several more.

Almost without exception the freight dock workers were unaware of the hazards of the material and the regulations restricting the amount that could be loaded on a plane. On one freight dock there were stacks of packages totaling 600 TI that the workers were planning to load onto the next plane to Columbus.

Eckels and Dunn calculated that a load of 100 transport indexes stacked in the cargo bin could give the passengers or crew members sitting directly above, a dose of 50 millirem or more an hour. On a four-hour flight, this dosage would total 200 millirem, or more than the 170 millirem figure that the Atomic Energy Commission has established as the maximum permissible dosage to a member of the general public *in a full year*.

The two captains discussed their findings with FAA officials, with the manufacturers of the pharmaceuticals that made up most of the radioactive loads, and with the Atomic Energy Commission, but to little effect.

"We used to compare ourselves to the farmer in a Frankenstein movie who has seen the monster," Dunn recalled recently. "We saw the monster out there but nobody would believe us. 'I don't see anything,' people would say. But it was there."

Finally in December of 1971 the two captains presented their findings to the House subcommittee on government operations, chaired by Congressman Jack Brooks of Texas. They showed their pictures and gave their tabulations of radioactive loads to the committee.

Committee members expressed concern, but FAA officials assured the committee that the situation was being taken care of. The FAA consulted with airline management officials and the AEC and on February 14, 1972, issued a "clarification" of the rule governing the shipment of radioactive material that actually allowed more material to be carried, and a greater legal exposure of passenger and crew.

Physicists at Washington University in St. Louis calculated that the legal dosage to the reproductive organs of a seated passenger or stewardess had been increased by the "clarification" from 5.5 millirem an hour to 18.1. Eckles and Dunn joined in a lawsuit filed by Ralph Nader's Aviation Consumer Action Project to force FAA to hold public hearings as required for any rule change. The new "interpretation" was clearly a new rule.

Meanwhile, Eckels and Dunn were becoming concerned with what was happening to the stewardesses on their airline. It's a small line, and just about everyone knows everyone else. During the first months of 1972 a number of their stewardess friends were having problem pregnancies.

"It got to the point," said Eckels, "when it seemed that every time a stewardess was pregnant something would go wrong." Was it possible that there was a connection between the high level of radioactivity that the stewardesses were being exposed to and the problem pregnancies?

There was no question that they were being exposed. On one flight Laurie Eckels, Captain Eckels' wife and a stewardess for the same airline, found that she was expected to prop up her feet on an illegal shipment of radioactive material with a transport index of 8. She got off the plane, phoned her husband who phoned the St. Louis office of the FAA, and the package was removed.

Eckels and Dunn kept track of each pregnancy of a stewardess on the airline for the full twelve months of 1972 and the first two months of 1973. Altogether, ten stewardesses became pregnant. Of that number, five had miscarriages or their children were born dead. Four had normal children and one had a deformed child. One stewardess had six miscarriages that year, and Eckels determined that she had flown regularly on a Friday morning flight with a heavy shipment of radioactive material.

A study of only ten pregnancies was not enough to establish scientifically that there was any connection between the radiation exposure and problem births. Other factors, such as the increased amount of cosmic radiation received at high altitudes, or conditions of work might be involved. But the problem births were certainly cause for concern.

A follow-up survey sent to all the stewardess chapters of ALPA was inconclusive. Some of the locals failed to respond, and several that did respond to the questionnaire gave vague information. The scattered results did indicate that the rate of problem births was much lower than the 50 percent recorded at the one airline. But certain airlines in certain locations appeared to be having a number of problem births.

Altogether, seventeen miscarriages and two children born with birth defects were reported on the other lines. One council simply reported eight problems. Again, the results are inconclusive, but they indicate a serious need for further study.

This is all the more true since the existing medical evidence shows that stewardesses are being exposed to excessive doses of radiation that would be expected to have effects on their children.

In 1960, James F. Crow, professor of genetics at the University of Wisconsin School of Medicine and president of the Genetics Society of Medicine, described the effects of low levels of radiation:

"Geneticists are convinced that there is no threshold for radiation-induced mutations," he wrote. "That is, there is no dose so low that it produced no mutations at all. Each dose, however small, that reaches the germ cells between conception and reproduction carries a risk to future generations proportional to the dose."

Alice Stewart and G. W. Kneale wrote in a research report published in the authoritative medical journal *Lancet* in June of 1970 that exposure of the fetus in the first three months of pregnancy to 80 to 100 millirems from an X-ray of the mother doubles the incidence of cancer in childhood.

John W. Gofman and Arthur R. Tamplin, former research scientists at the Atomic Energy Commission's Lawrence Radiation Laboratory in Livermore, California, testified before the Senate Public Works Committee on Air and Water Pollution on November 18, 1969, that the allowable radiation dosage for the general public should be reduced from the current 170 millirems a year to 17. They based their recommendation in part on research findings that radioactive fallout amounting to 100 millirems had perceptibly affected the number of deaths per

1,000 live births in upper New York State. They stated in their testimony before the committee:

"We wish to apprise you that in our opinion, the most crucial pressing problem facing everyone concerned with any and all burgeoning atomic energy activities is to secure the earliest possible revision downward by at least a factor of tenfold of the allowable radiation dosage to the population from peaceful atomic energy activities."

And yet with all these indications of serious health hazards, from February 14, 1972, until October 1, 1973, stewardesses and passengers could be legally exposed to 18 millirem an hour without their knowledge or consent. It would take only ten hours of flying time with a legally packed load to exceed the 170 millirem limit established by the AEC for a yearly dosage, and only one hour of flying time to exceed the yearly dosage limit proposed by Gofman and Tamplin.

Since October 1, 1973, the legal limits have reverted to 5.5 millirem an hour. But this still means that a stewardess could theoretically be exposed to 4,950 millirems a year in her 900 hours of flying, which is almost thirty times the 170 millirem limit.

To make matters worse, the FAA has little machinery to enforce its rules, and radioactive cargoes are still routinely shipped at several times the legal limits, according to the ALPA hazardous materials committee. The AEC itself confirmed this fact in a study conducted from May to August of 1973 at four major airports.

At Logan Airport in Boston, for example, even though the pharmaceutical companies, airline officials, and dock loaders were all alerted that a study was being made, thirteen of the shipments measured by Geiger counter in the plane cabin showed readings of over 10 millirem an hour at passenger seat level.

This incredible carelessness with human life has apparently been allowed to develop for several reasons: the great increase in recent years of products made from radioactive wastes; the pressures applied by the air carriers on the FAA to maximize profits in what had until recently been a flagging cargo business; and the traditional stance of the Atomic Energy Commission, which as both promoter and regulator of nuclear development, consistently downplays or ignores health hazards caused by radioactivity.

The National Transportation Safety Board estimated in its report on an accident involving a spill of radioactive material that as of 1971 there were from 3 to 4 million patients treated with radioactive isotopes and that an unknown amount of products were used industrially in radiography, measuring devices, self-illuminating devices, and isotopic power devices. The NTSB estimated that the air shipments of isotopes that year involving pharmaceutical products only were in the range of from 300,000 to 540,000.

"The majority of these shipments," the report stated, "is believed to travel on regularly scheduled passenger carrying aircraft." This is because most of these isotopes have a relatively short "half life," and a rapid rate of decay.

In 1970, the report said, there were 464 air shipments

of special nuclear material such as enriched uranium reactor fuel. Three airlines transported 90 percent of these shipments that year, the NTSB report said.

The report was unable to give an overall estimate for the number of nonpharmaceutical radioactive shipments, but it noted that the nuclear industry had an annual growth rate of 15 percent, and the radiopharmaceutical field a rate of 25 percent a year.

Using these estimates, approximately one out of every ten passenger flight would be expected to be carrying some form of radioactivity. Some estimates are much higher. Ralph Nader's Aviation Consumer Action Project has petitioned the FAA to ban the shipments altogether until it could demonstrate it was capable of regulating them. The petition estimated that 25 percent of all passenger flights carried radioactive loads.

These shipments are being made under regulations that were formulated in the 1950's, when the transportation of radioactivity was a rare event. In fact, the original guidelines were established with the idea that a passenger could be expected to receive a radioactive dose only once in a lifetime.

There are some legitimate differences of opinion about the exact effects of low level doses of radiation, but no impartial observer, when apprised of the facts, could contend that there is not an urgent need to change the regulations governing how much radiation the passengers and crew of airplanes are being subjected to.

Neil McBride, an attorney for Ralph Nader's Aviation

Consumer Action Project, asked some leading atomic experts to comment on the situation.

Karl Z. Morgan, director of the Health-Physics Division of the Oak Ridge National Laboratory, president emeritus of the Radiation Protection Association, and one of the most respected physicists in the AEC, replied to McBride on July 26, 1972.

"On September 1, 1947, I was appointed a member of a Subcommittee on Shipment of Radioactive Materials of the Committee on Radioactivity of the National Research Council," Morgan wrote, "and helped to frame the first regulations for the shipping of radioisotopes. These recommendations became the basis for shipping standards not only in the United States but throughout the world."

Morgan noted that during the past ten years he has carried a film badge and a Geiger counter when he flew in order to get some idea of how much radioactivity passengers were being exposed to.

Only in the past two years had he noticed significant doses, he said, and "on several occasions the doses have been equal to or greater than those we estimated would be delivered to a passenger no more than once in a lifetime when we first established these regulations."

"In fact," the letter continues, "at that time the regulations were not so designed that it would be impossible for a passenger to receive too much dose, but rather that the probability of such an exposure would be exceedingly low. It turns out that a passenger who travels or commutes

between certain cities might receive close to this maximum dose (the dose anticipated no more than in one
flight in a lifetime) on every flight."

Dr. Morgan's concern is all the more alarming when
you consider that he states in his letter that he had never
encountered any illegal doses, and was speaking only of
doses that are legal under the present regulations.

He recommends revising the table of distances and the
amount of radioactive materials permitted on passenger
planes so that exposure to passengers and crew would be
limited to 1 or 2 millirem an hour. He notes in a round-
about way, that under current regulations crew members
should be listed as radiation workers, required to wear
radioactivity-exposure badges, and limited in their flying
time.

There is an almost comical note to the letter when this
elderly gentleman, who helped formulate the original
rules, described his first encounter with a high dose on a
flight from New York to Knoxville in November of 1971.

"I was rather shocked when I entered the plane in
New York to observe by my personal radiation monitor
in my pocket which started chirping rapidly, that apparently there was radiation being emitted. As I approached
my assigned seat, I noted the chirping frequency continued to increase, and I asked the stewardess if I could
change my seat. She asked why, and without thinking I
stated that the radiation level was too high.

"She raised her eyebrows (as if to say another intoxi-
cated crackpot), but since the plane was not crowded,
she gave me a seat in the tail of the plane where the dose

rate was much lower. After the plane reached altitude, I called the stewardess and showed her my Geiger counter, and she was most interested in listening to the chirps indicating the presence of radioisotopes on the plane. I suggested, perhaps the captain might be equally interested, and she asked him to come back and see what I had. His first reaction was, 'You mean there is radiation on my plane? I don't want any of it.'

"I told him the radiation dose rate was within the permissible limit, but in some parts of the plane it was higher than I thought should be permitted except on very exceptional and unusual cases."

Dr. Morgan and the pilot spent much of the remainder of the flight secretly taking measurements in different parts of the plane. The highest readings they found were 2 millirem an hour at seat level in four seats.

Of course, we are not all fortunate enough to carry a Geiger counter in our pocket and be able to change seats when it chirps. But the most interesting aspect of this story is that Dr. Morgan asked to change his seat, and considered that the doses should only be permitted in "very exceptional and unusual cases" as a result of a 2 millirem per hour reading. That is less than half the legal dosage under existing regulations.

And when the Atomic Energy Commission had a test conducted during May and June of 1973 at Boston's Logan Airport, forty-seven of the sixty-two flights checked had considerably higher levels of radiation at seat level than the amount that so disturbed Dr. Morgan. One wonders what his reaction would have been to the readings of 15, 17.5, and 20.2 millirem per hour obtained in that study. These readings are all the more frightening since the freight loaders and company officials were alerted that a survey was being conducted, and presumably exercised extra caution.

For a long time it was thought that there was a threshold below which low levels of radiation would have no harmful effects. This threshold was constantly lowered over the years. In 1934, the International Commission on Radiological Protection considered that radiation workers could be exposed to a maximum of 1,000 millirem a week. In 1950 this was lowered to 300 millirem, and in 1956 to 100 millirem. Finally, in 1965, the ICRP determined that "any exposure to radiation may carry some risks for the development of somatic effects, including leukemia and other malignancies, and of hereditary effects. The assumption is made that, down to the lowest levels of dose, the risk of inducing disease or disability increases with the dose accumulated by the individual. This assumption implies that there is no wholly safe dose of radiation . . . Any exposure to radiation is assumed to entail a risk of deleterious effects."

Several of the nation's leading scientists had warned that this was the case, that radiation exposure was apparently linear and cumulative, with no absolutely safe dosage, and no threshold. Gofman and Tamplin came to this conclusion while working for the AEC on the possible effects of radiation on the public, and recommended in 1969 that the limits of exposure be revised downward from 170 millirem to 17 millirem a year.

But the AEC repudiated its own experts and to this day continues to minimize the dangers involved in exposure. This AEC position received a jolt in November of 1972 when the National Academy of Science's advisory committee on the Biological Effects of Ionizing Radiation lent its prestige to the belief that the effects of low level radiation are cumulative and dangerous.

The BEIR report based its conclusion on studies dating back to 1948, linking low level radiation exposure and slight increases among the general population in the incidence of leukemia and cancer.

In 1971, Hermann J. Schaefer, head of the biophysics division of the Naval Aerospace Medical Research Laboratory in Pensacola, Florida, reported in *Science Magazine* on the possible effects of cosmic radiation in supersonic planes. He argued that the dangers were insignificant.

Figuring that the total cosmic exposure would equal 500 millirem a year, he wrote that the increased chances for leukemia would be only 1 percent, and the life shortening effects would be only 1.4 percent a year, a "marginal enhancement of risk." He did recommend, however, that SST crew members be classified as "radiation workers" and monitored for exposure. He was not including, of course, the radiation dosage from the cargo bin.

There are also the dangers of radioactive "spills" on board planes, and of the possible effects of radioactivity after a plane crash. A spill occurred on December 31, 1971, aboard a Delta Air Lines plane. A quantity of radioactivity leaked from a bulk shipment, while the shipment was enroute from the manufacturer in Tuxedo, New York, to Houston, Texas.

The National Transportation Safety Board said in its report that the plane "was contaminated and 917 passengers had traveled aboard it before discovery of the leakage and removal of the aircraft from service."

Some passengers were exposed to between 400 and 1,000 millirems as a result of that leak, according to calculations made by ALPA. Agents who unloaded the leaking shipments were exposed to several times that amount.

When Congressman Brooks held hearings on the subject in the spring of 1972, FAA officials conceded that the shipment was illegal because of the number of transport indexes and the distance from the cargo bin to the passenger cabin. The FAA officials also conceded that the regular shipments from this company that had been transported each week for the twelve months prior to the accident, had all been illegal.

There is no recorded incident of radioactive leakage after a plane crash. But investigators for the National Transportation Safety Board conceded that they now carry Geiger counters when they approach the scene of a crash.

These radioactive materials should be removed entirely from passenger aircraft, as is called for in the lawsuit filed by Nader's Aviation Consumer Action Project.

At the very least, the type three, or "Radioactive Yellow III" shipments should be banned from passenger aircraft. The Types I and II shipments involve one-half a millirem or less exposure at a distance of three feet, and it is only the category III shipments that present serious problems.

But even with the best of regulations, something will have to be done about the way that the Federal Aviation Administration fails to enforce the law.

Congressman Brooks concluded after hearings held on the question in June of 1972: "There is an almost unbelievable web of deficiencies and unsound procedures surrounding the packing and shipment of radioactive materials by air."

The situation had not improved by the spring of 1973.

"With each year that passes," he said then, "our country witnesses an alarming increase in the exposure of our nation's citizens to potential and actual tragedies involving shipments of highly dangerous and poisonous materials.

"Our system of regulating the shipment of hazardous materials by air is totally out of control."

Until something is done, every stewardess should be equipped with her own Geiger counter. Passengers might want to carry them also.

The Future of a Sex Object

WHEN I take a flight these days it is hard to believe that I was ever a stewardess. There is the tough, reassuring voice of the captain over the intercom. There are the stewardesses, having to smile, having to meet my eyes, having to try to act subservient.

It seems like a distant life in a previous incarnation. I was someone else then.

Things have opened up a lot for women over the past several years, but in 1968 when I joined the airlines it seemed that, unless for some exceptional reason you had prepared yourself since early adolescence for a different role, you would end up in one of the "women's" occupations.

You could become a waitress, a teacher, a secretary, or a nurse. Then there were the "glamor" jobs for the chosen few: entertainer, model, airline stewardess, Playboy Bunny. Most women's jobs seem to have some elements of neurosis built in, but the extent to which a woman is expected to fulfill a sexual myth varies from job to job. And so does the degree to which she's expected to be subservient to her male boss, whether he's a doctor, captain, or manager.

Last summer I took some classes at the University of Illinois and met a number of women who were in one of these careers or another before quitting and going back to school. We compared notes and some of the similarities were amazing.

One of my friends became a Playboy Bunny the same year that I became a stewardess. She prepared herself carefully for her job interview, dolling herself up in white vinyl boots and knit minidress, and wore her long bleached blond hair down over one eye. She is six feet tall and at the time weighed just 120 pounds, so she must have been quite a sight. When she walked in for her interview the cameras started going off. She was selected to illustrate a story they were doing on the opening of a new Playboy hotel.

Playboy bunnies also have very precise instructions on how to act at all times. For instance when she was not busy serving drinks she was supposed to lean back against anything convenient—a piano or a wall, with legs crossed, one hand on her hip. She was evaluated on such matters.

She quit after nine months, feeling totally disillusioned and degraded. Nine months, it seems, is longer than average for a bunny. Her hair is its natural brown now, and she wears it in a casual shag. She wears very little makeup anymore. But she is at ease with herself. She

knows who she is now, and that has virtually nothing to
do with how strangers perceive her.

Being a stewardess differs from other women's jobs
only in degree. But it seems all the more bizarre a voca-
tion in 1974, when women are becoming lawyers and
doctors and even semi truck and cab drivers, and men
are becoming stewards and telephone operators and
nurses.

When I was growing up I thought that to be a woman
meant to be passive. I didn't feel passive, and my sexual
identity felt threatened. So I picked women's jobs with
uniforms: first a nurse, then a stewardess. I wore a costume so that I would know I was a woman, so that every
one could see I was playing a woman's role. I hid behind
the uniform and displayed myself as safely passive.

When I became disillusioned with flying, I was filled
with self-doubt. The airlines encourage this kind of doubt,
always assuring us that we are the most fortunate of
women. If we find our job perplexing and irritating, does
that mean we are not natural women?

Jan Taylor feels that often women who are least comfortable in the passive feminine role internalize it the
most, to ease self-doubts about their sexual identity.

"She gets the message that she must be crazy to want
something else and her doubt tends to make her throw
herself into the female role."

Jan feels that this is what happened to her, and I think
it was similar in my case. I was very close to my three
brothers growing up, and I remember how bitter I was
when they talked of professions and accomplishing things

in the world, and my sister and I were supposed to become suburban mothers.

"If she is pretty," Jan continues, "this will eventually compound her dilemma, because she can play the female game and win. As she continues to get reinforced for the role, she gets deeper and deeper into it, and the conflict between herself and her role becomes more intense.

"The result is a deeply frustrated and confused individual. But once she frees herself from the prison of the female role, and gets in touch with her true self, she is liable to become a walking dynamo. She will experience a radical metamorphosis."

That is certainly what happened in Jan's case, and in the case of other activists that I have met through Stewardesses For Women's Rights.

I think this process is just beginning to happen to me. I am still working through the whole experience. I'm twenty-eight years old and I'm just beginning to grow. My peers in school are nineteen. I feel those five years of flying were almost dead space in my life.

I am still discovering things that I had blacked out for years.

My husband and I have moved to Los Angeles, and one Saturday a·few weeks ago I arranged to meet Jan Taylor during her layover on a flight from Chicago. It was her last flight, and we planned a kind of celebration. I was standing in the lobby of the Airport Marina, waiting for Jan to arrive, when this large businessman in his forties walked up, stood very close to me, and made this sucking noise, as if perhaps calling a squirrel.

"Hi there, baby!" he said.

I just moaned, "Oh, no," turned my back on him, and walked away. It really felt strange to be mistaken for a stewardess, and to find myself in that same old silly ritual.

Jan finally arrived and we spent some six hours talking over coffee in a restaurant near the hotel. Several stewardess friends came and went during the course of the day. I started telling Jan how strange it felt to be back in the stewardess world, and then something popped into my mind that had been blocked out for well over a year.

I suddenly remembered one time while I was a stewardess when my pent-up hostility showed itself. I must have blocked out the memory because it was unacceptable behavior, and I still have a hard time recalling the exact circumstances.

A man had been badgering all the stewardesses on this flight. He was drunk and obnoxious. He grabbed at me several times as I walked past, and I think I was pulling away from him while he was grappling with me when he shouted out:

"You're all goddamn whores anyway."

He made me feel like less than nothing. I was suddenly overcome with a deep rage. I grabbed his tie with my right hand, pulling it toward me, and held my left hand against his Adam's apple. I wanted to strangle him.

"I don't want to hear another word out of you," I muttered at him. I still don't remember what happened after that, but I think he was quiet for the rest of the trip.

My husband and I live in a house on the ocean in

Malibu. I never used to like being alone, but now I really enjoy being out of sight of the city.

Our marriage has changed, as I have developed my own identity, but this identity is much stronger now. This is the first time I have felt like I am home.

I am doing some work for the local chapter of the Stewardesses For Women's Rights, because it helped me and my friends so much in coming to terms with our lives.

We are fighting for a whole series of changes that would permit some dignity and self-respect in the job. The suggestive advertising and image-making should be done away with; stewardesses should be federally licensed, like other members of the flight crew; a condition of licensing should be increased training in safety and medical aid; more dignified uniforms should be introduced; opportunities for promotions and transfers should be opened up; elaborate meals and fashion shows that exhaust the crew should be eliminated; drinking should be limited; safety standards should be established for seating arrangements of the flight attendants; hazardous materials should be eliminated from the cargo bins of passenger planes. . . .

The list could go on.

These reforms would not deprive passengers of a pleasant trip. They would not impose an impossible hardship on the airline companies. Passengers could still be pleasantly entertained in other, less exploitive ways. But these kinds of changes will not come about easily. They will have to be fought for and won by the stewards and stewardesses themselves, collectively breaking through the corporate neurosis.

A lot of people feel threatened by the changing sexual roles of the 1970's. But in a technological society the divisions of labor can be nothing but arbitrarily drawn. Our modern-day roles are not clarified by repeating to ourselves over and over again the myths of the American frontier. They can only be further confused by the commercial exploitation of sex.

Increasingly women are refusing to accept the role of passive, submissive, subservient woman. It seems the submissive woman pays the price of trying to play an impossible role and in later life tends to try to get revenge on her husband for the sacrifices of self she has made. The husband in turn tries to escape from this domestic hell into a safe, adolescent dream world where there are young girls who are not people, but simply passive, eager bodies—the Playboy Bunnies and the airline stewardesses of our modern mythology.

We used to discuss these matters in the cafeteria at the University of Illinois: a former stewardess, a former Playboy Bunny, a former waitress, a former housewife, and an active philosophy professor. One thing that we discovered was that we could be friends, that we didn't have to orient our whole lives toward men. Another thing we discovered was that we could no longer be intimidated by threats to our sexual identity, or accusations that we were radical. We are doing what so many other people are doing in the 1970's—trying to understand what playing out the traditional feminine role has done to us and where we go from here.

Doing away with the mythology is not such a frightening prospect if you think about it. If to be a flight attendant was to belong to a profession of men and women, licensed by the federal government, with improved standards for safety and with the kind of job security and advancement opportunities common to most professions, it could be a reasonable way of life.

The airlines would collectively hide their faces in their hands at the very thought. But if they peered out between their fingers they would see that, miraculously, people were still flying airplanes. In fact service was improved, because stewards and stewardesses had pride in their profession and, no longer having to act out an essentially neurotic script, were healthier people. Safety was greatly improved, because flight attendants were better trained, more experienced, and had more say about potential dangers.

That is what it would be like if the airlines can be persuaded to step through the looking glass back into the real world.